conte

Published by City Magazines Ltd, Aldwych House,
81 Aldwych, London W.C.2, England. Printed and bound
in England by Jarrold & Sons Ltd, Norwich.
© 1971 City Magazines Ltd.
SBN 7235 0093 2

62½np
12/6

STAR TREK
CAPTIVES IN SPACE

UNDER THE COMMAND OF CAPTAIN JAMES T. KIRK, THE MASSIVE STARSHIP 'ENTERPRISE' HUNG MOTIONLESS IN SPACE ABOVE THE ATMOSPHERE OF A PREVIOUSLY UNCHARTED PLANET...

IT'S INHABITED, CAPTAIN. I'M GETTING A REPLY TO MY CALL-SIGN!

OKAY, LIEUTENANT. ACTIVATE TRANSLATORS AND TELL THEM WE'RE ON A FRIENDLY CONTACT MISSION!

WELCOME TO SKUR, EARTHMEN. OUR RULER REQUESTS YOU SEND A DELEGATION AT ONCE. WE WILL GIVE YOU A COURSE TO FOLLOW...

MINUTES LATER, KIRK, HIS FIRST OFFICER MR. SPOCK, AND CHIEF ENGINEER SCOTT STOOD READY IN THE MATTER-TRANSPORTER TUBES...

INSTANTLY, THEY RE-MATERIALIZED ON THE SURFACE OF SKUR...

LOOKS A WELL CIVILIZED PLACE. BUT THERE'S NO ONE TO MEET US!

5

8

9

SPACE FLEET

It's blast-off for America's Apollo 11 space-flight, as the powerful Saturn launch vehicle departs for the moon.

"**M**ission control to flight commander. All systems screened. Prepare for countdown . . ."

The brief seconds ticked away as nerves tensed like bow-strings. Control-room technicians and astronauts alike exchanged anxious glances.

Suddenly, amid a billowing cloud of fire, the sleek, needle-shaped rocket rose majestically into the atmosphere. Behind it, the gantry was enveloped in incredible heat.

"Take-off procedure completed. Mooncraft on course and going well!"

Relieved grins eased taut faces as the small army of ground control experts turned to the complex of tracking equipment about them.

Yet *another* space-launching had been completed successfully.

*   *   *

Man has already stepped out on the moon's surface. But he has only been able to undertake such an amazing space-journey because of the *rocket*.

But just like the many various models of motor-car which ever pour on to the world's highways so, too, are there different types of rockets; each designed and constructed for a particular type of space mission.

The American NASA (National Aeronautics and Space Administration) space programme employs a range of launch vehicles of varying sizes and capabilities.

In the scale drawing (right) you can see just some of them:

Scout This is a four-stage solid-fuel rocket that can place a 240 lb. satellite in orbit about 300 miles above the Earth. 72 feet tall, it is used to launch small scientific satellites and for re-entry studies.

An Italian San Marco satellite is launched in the United States by a Scout rocket.

Thor-Agena D A two-stage, 76 foot vehicle, it is capable of placing 1,600 lb. of equipment in a 300 mile orbit. It is used to launch orbiting observatories, and large scientific and applications satellites.

Delta This highly-successful, three-stage rocket stands 90 feet tall, and can place 880 lb. of equipment into Earth orbit. It is also capable of sending a probe to the moon or a craft to Mars or Venus. Delta rockets can also launch a series of various satellites.

Atlas-Agena D 104 feet high, this is a two-stage rocket capable of placing 600 lb. of equipment in a 300 mile orbit. Its uses also include lunar probes, the Mariner missions to Mars and Venus, and for positioning the heavier orbiting observatories. This rocket also boosted the Gemini rendezvous target vehicles into Earth orbit.

Atlas-Centaur Comprising an Atlas first stage and a Centaur second stage, it stands 117 feet tall and can put 9,900 lb. of equipment into Earth orbit. It can also launch spacecraft of varying sizes to the moon, Mars or Venus.

Titan 2 The Gemini launch vehicle, it stands 120 feet high, and can place a spacecraft into orbit round the Earth. Due to it using a liquid propellant that can be stored indefinitely, it can be fuelled well ahead of a launch.

Saturn 1 This is a two-stage rocket, 190 feet high. It is capable of orbiting a spacecraft weighing 10 tons. It is used for unmanned flights in the Apollo programme.

Uprated Saturn 1 Its first stage is similar to that of Saturn 1, but has slightly more thrust. The second stage is bigger and more powerful, enabling the rocket to place 20 tons of equipment into Earth orbit. It stands 225 feet high.

Saturn 5 This is the most powerful launch vehicle in the NASA programme. The rocket for the moon missions, it has three stages and is 364 feet high. It is capable of placing 142 tons of equipment into a low Earth orbit and sending spacecraft to the moon's surface.

This time, it's take-off for America's Apollo 12, using a Saturn lunar mission launch vehicle.

A three-stage Delta launch vehicle noses spacebound to launch an Orbiting Solar Observatory.

GEMINI-TITAN 2   SATURN 5

DELTA   ATLAS-AGENA D

UPRATED SATURN 1

SCOUT   SATURN 1

AS-CENTAUR

THOR-AGENA D

6′

DANGEROUS LINE

LAND OF THE GIANTS

Captain Steve Burton held up a hand, halting Mark Wilson as they made their difficult way through the great forest. Mark's eyes moved in the direction that Steve was pointing and he saw the familiar notice demanding the capture of the Little People.

Ever since their spaceship, code-named 'Spendthrift', had shattered a time and space barrier to land on the giant planet, they had been in constant danger from the giants who were baited by the huge reward offered by the authorities for the arrest of the Earth-people.

Suddenly, behind them, came the ominous rustling of leaves and the crack of dry twigs. Was this another attempt to curtail their freedom in the forest that they had made their home?

Steve and Mark held their breath as they hid behind a giant mushroom. But then they sighed with relief; the approaching figure was not a giant. It was Dan Bailey, Steve's Negro co-pilot:

"Quickly, Steve," Dan rasped out as he tried to get his breath back. "A giant took Barry."

Barry Lockridge was the youngest member of the stranded party and with his dog, Chipper, provided much of the amusement to keep the others in high spirits.

"What happened?" asked Mark, the lines of worry furrowing his brow. "He went for a walk with Chipper."

"Yes, I know, and a giant in some sort of uniform caught him. Chipper's barking warned us, but we were too late to help."

"Come on!" Steve was rushing through the trees towards camp. Valerie and Betty were near to tears as they watched him snatch up the homing device that covered a ten mile radius, indicating the position of the camp.

Leaving Fitzhugh to look after the girls, Steve, Mark and Dan followed after Chipper as the dog barked excitedly through the forest, uncannily aware that they were going to look for his young master.

As they ran, Mark drew Steve's attention to the reward poster they had looked at only minutes before. The notice fluttered in the breeze, partially torn from the nails that held the corners.

"That giant must have done it," suggested Mark with a frown. "Now why should he want to tear a reward poster? Maybe he's got some grudge against the authorities."

"Keep hoping so, Mark," Steve said quietly. "Maybe Barry won't end up in the hands of the police after all."

They resumed the chase, desperately urging their legs to go faster.

Then they stopped abruptly. Ahead, was the main road to town and parked by the forest edge was a giant car.

"Is that the man?" Steve asked Dan, indicating an old giant who was opening the car door.

"That's him, Steve. What are you going to do?"

"I don't know—try to reason with him I guess."

Steve knew that it was a wild scheme. Not many giants could resist the high price on the heads of the Earth-people.

"What do you make of the uniform, Mark?" Steve's pulse skipped a beat as he remembered the times he had been held in the clutches of the giant authorities.

"I don't recognize it," Mark muttered as they moved from cover towards the giant car.

Steve cupped his hands to his mouth. "Hey! Old man!" he shouted, and the giant looked about him, not appreciating where the sound had originated.

"Down here!" bellowed Steve, and with a start the giant glanced down. His expression changed from surprise to delight and his greying moustache seemed to bristle as his face came nearer to the little trio.

"You've got a friend of ours," explained Steve, knowing that the words sounded hollow and weak. "What do you want with him?"

The giant ignored the question and before they could flee, a gnarled hand encircled Steve, Mark and Dan and they were lifted high into the air.

Chipper barked excitedly but was soon whining miserably as he saw the car speeding away with his friends securely held captive within.

The three men found Barry frightened, but fit and well, pressed against the side of the cardboard box in which they had been placed. The box was quite large with holes cut in the lid and reminded Steve of the type of box he used to keep snails and caterpillars in when he was a boy.

"Where is he taking us?" Mark's question hung in the air for a moment, none of the others prepared to guess at the giant's plans.

"Get on my shoulders, Steve," suggested Dan, crouching down. "Maybe you can see something through the holes in the lid."

Teetering beneath Steve's weight, Dan straightened up and moved the captain to the top of the box.

"Yes I can see out," Steve called down to the others. "Hey, we're slowing down—we're at some sort of garage."

Everything Steve saw appeared to be so massive that it was difficult to identify buildings except from great distances. Then he saw a notice board.

"No, it's not a garage. We're at Wickford Railroad Depot."

Steve dropped to the floor of the box, his face showing the signs of relief that he felt.

"This giant is a railroad worker—he's taking us to work with him."

"How do you know he won't hand us over to the police?" Mark was less optimistic than Steve.

"If he wanted to do that he wouldn't have come to this place, would he?" insisted Steve. "I reckon he plans to keep us."

"Did he say anything to you, Barry?"

Dan asked placing an encouraging hand on the boy's shoulder.

"Yes. I've been trying to make sense of it. He said that I was just right to fit into the railway."

"But, that's *ridiculous*. You'd be okay for a giant's model railway, but not the real thing." As Mark said the words he realized that he could be close to the reason for their capture.

Next minute, they were no longer in any doubt. The giant raised the lid of the box and his not unpleasant face grinned down at them.

"Now Johnny will have a driver, a guard, a station master *and* a porter," muttered the huge man. "He will be so pleased with his old grandpop."

Once more the lid closed and the Earth-people felt the violent movements that told them they were being carried out of the car and into the open.

Steve tried to detect the noises which crowded in around them—the hiss of steam, the clanking of metal on metal. A shrill whistle and then the shrill sound of a klaxon hooter made them realize they were in the midst of the railway marshalling yard.

"We're going aboard a train!" Steve was forced to shout as the sound of diesel motors revving to a high pitch came from all round. "We're in the cab of an engine."

The motor died to a gentle purr and then they were flung off their feet as the whole box shuddered forwards.

"The train's moving," cried Barry, trying to clamber up from the floor of the box.

Steve tried to comfort the boy as he felt the train gathering speed.

"I'm fed up with being cooped up in this shoe-box," he suddenly yelled. "We've a chance now. Dan, Mark—give me a hand."

Steve had taken the precaution of bringing the hatchet they had made from a matchstick and a broken razor blade. It had become standard equipment whenever they ventured from the camp and luckily the giant had not noticed it when he captured them.

He took a wild swing at the wall of the box and the sharp blade dug firmly into the thick card. Mark was by Steve's side at once, trying to free the blade so that they could widen the cut.

Barry stifled a laugh as the blade came clear suddenly, sending Mark

---

. . . A gnarled hand encircled Steve, Mark and Dan and they were lifted high up into the air.

and Steve flying to the opposite wall.

"It's all right for you to laugh," smiled Steve, realizing how funny they must have looked. "But this matchstick's heavy!"

For half an hour they took it in turns to swing the make-shift hatchet at the widening split in the cardboard box. Then they could see out. The old man sat with his back to them, driving the diesel shunter.

A younger companion was beside the old man, checking the pressure dials and controls systems of the locomotive.

The train was not moving fast and Mark quickly noted that they were probably shifting freight from Wickford Yard to the main line.

"That could mean the engine will be going back to Wickford," finished Mark, a ray of hope brightening his eyes.

"Well, we can get out of this box at least," smiled Steve, stepping through the opening.

There were a thousand hiding places in the grimy cab of the engine. Steve inched his way nearer to the door of the cab. He could just manage to see the rapidly passing railway buildings and sleepers as he looked through the ill-fitting door. The clackity-clack of the steel wheels on the rails vibrated through the cab to every bone in his body as he desperately tried to think of a method of escape.

Supposing Mark was wrong? Supposing the train didn't go back to the depot at Wickford? They would be miles from camp with an impossible journey back to the others.

"What you doing tonight, pop?" Steve heard the younger railman ask. "Playing with your trains again?"

There was a note of derision in the youth's voice and Steve felt a moment of sorrow for the old man.

"There's nothing wrong with building model railways for your grandson, is there?" The old man asked the question with a tremor in his voice as he tried to overcome his embarrassment. "I'm going to fix that railway so that it's the best in the whole country."

"I know all that, pop," persisted the youth, "but you spend all day on trains, shunting these trucks and wagons from Wickford to Stansby, Stansby to Chalfont. Don't you get tired of the sight of sleepers and signals?"

Mark heard the conversation, too. He moved nearer to Steve.

"It seems this is a regular run for them. That means they *must* be going back to the depot later."

"Yes, but how much later? What happens when that lad goads the old man into revealing that he's got us aboard?"

"I don't think that's likely. He wouldn't risk telling anyone else—not if he means to keep us."

"I don't know—the old man's proud. He could try to prove his point about the best model railway in the country. I doubt if there's another with a crew like us."

Mark saw the sense of Steve's words and as he watched the old man getting more excited about his grandson and their toy trains, the captain's fears seemed to be fully justified.

"What are we going to do?" Mark asked the question in desperation. He had spent a long time trying to come up with a solution to their predicament, but had failed.

"We've got to get off this train," replied Steve. "Okay, maybe it will return to Wickford—but when? What if the old man lives in Chalfont. Maybe he'll take us home when he gets to the end of the line and we'll be shut away in some garden shed with nothing but toy trains for company. No, we can't risk hanging about. We've got to get off."

"We could cause a diversion," suggested Dan, carefully moving round an oil puddle to join Steve and Mark. "Those pressure tubes up there are made of rubber. The hatchet would cut through them like a knife through butter."

"Fine," enthused Mark. "If we hit the right one the oil pressure will drop and the train will slow to a stop."

"Then what?" Steve had a plan forming in his mind, but it was full of danger, and if one of the others could come up with something better, he would be happy to abandon his idea.

There was an exchange of tight-lipped glances from one to the other. Steve shrugged. There was nothing left for it. They would have to take the risks.

"Right," whispered Steve grimly as he saw the old man look pointedly round at the cardboard box. "We'll wait till the train reaches a station—some place where we can get on a train back to Wickford. Then we'll cut the pressure tube and slide down the sand pipe to the tracks."

"That means we'll be right under the wheels," gasped Dan.

Steve nodded slowly. To them the ground was some sixty feet below, he could think of no other way of travelling that tremendous distance.

"We're leaving a lot to chance," muttered Mark. "How are we going to know whether a train travelling the other way is going to Wickford. We could end up in a worse mess."

"Listen, Mark, we're in a tight spot. We have to take risks or we're finished. What do you think, Dan?"

Dan's eyes narrowed as all the dangers of the scheme flooded into his mind. He glanced at Barry who was out of earshot of the three men, then he gave a sharp nod of the head.

"I'll go along with the plan. I'll explain things to Barry. He'll have to come down the sand pipe on my back. He'd never make it alone."

Dan moved across the cab to Barry and Steve craned his neck to look round the door of the engine. The

incessant shuddering of the locomotive across the track joins had
vibrated the door ajar.

The wind whipped into his eyes as
the train lumbered on. Ahead he saw
the network of points and crossovers
that heralded a large junction. This
would be as good a spot as any to
take the gamble of escape.

"We're in luck," Steve told Mark as
he returned to the warmth of the cab. "I
think there's a station up ahead."

Mark eyed the thick rubber tube that
carried the oil to the pressure chambers
of the diesel's cylinders. It would be a
tough climb to reach the tube, but the
Little People had learned the hard
way that a normal task on Earth took
on superhuman proportions in this
hostile world of giants.

Without waiting to consult Steve, he
started to climb, using any available
foot and hand hold—bolts and screw
heads, rivets and congealed dry paint
—until he had taken up a comfortable
enough position to swing the small

but razor-sharp hatchet at the tube.

He drew in his breath, waiting for
Steve's signal indicating the right
moment, and prayed that the old man
and the youth would not take it upon
themselves to glance just a foot to
their right. If they did they could not fail
to see him.

Steve's upraised hand fell to slap his
thigh and Mark swung with all his
strength. He felt the sharp blade sink
into the rubber. He heard the hiss as
the oil started to seep through the
fracture. Then he was flying across the
cab, crashing headlong towards the
iron floor as the pressure shot the oil
in a thick black fountain of released
power.

It was Dan who saw the falling
figure. He didn't have to think about his
actions. He ran forward with his arms
outstretched.

The wind hissed through his
clenched teeth as Mark's weight hit
him and they went rolling over in the
skidding, filthy oil.

*Cutting through the box with a make-
shift hatchet, they saw the old man
driving the diesel shunter.*

For long moments they lay still,
the air rasping in the backs of their
throats. Then their dazed senses began
to clear. Steve was yelling at them,
waving his arms for them to follow him
as he edged his way out of the cab
door along the ridge of metal above
the churning, thundering wheels.

The pipe that carried sand down to
the line to enable the wheels to grip
the rails on gradients was the thick-
ness of his body as he slid inch by
inch towards the ground, far below.

Then the engine was slowing up
rapidly, the oil pressure draining from
the pistons and cylinders. Mark was
above Steve, sliding after the captain,
with Dan behind him, Barry holding
tightly to the co-pilot's back.

A dark shadow passed by Steve as
he saw the giant engine wheels slow to

15

a halt. Another train was coming alongside on the other track. It was also stopping for they were in the station.

He reached the rail and sighed with relief, knowing that they were safe from the pursuing wagons. They were at a standstill, presenting no threat. Mark had made certain of the pressure tube.

Dawn was approaching when Steve felt the warmth of the hot tea at the back of his throat. He looked up at the grinning faces of Mark and Dan.

"If you've got your breath back," came Valerie's pleasant voice, "perhaps you'll finish the story."

Steve still could not believe they were safely back at camp. For nearly thirteen hours they had been walking, trudging from Wickford Railroad Depot to the forest, watching the steadily flashing light of the homing device that was guiding them to the girls and Fitzhugh.

"The train ride back was quite comfortable. We found an empty first class compartment," Steve smiled, making light of the return journey from the unidentified station where they had left the broken-down diesel and the old man.

"Yes," agreed Mark. "We had a bit of a job climbing up the coach wheels and of course we were taking quite a risk that we wouldn't end up miles from Wickford, but maybe good fortune really does smile on the brave."

"I can't tell you how worried we've been," murmured Betty, taking Steve's cup and refilling it from the toy tea pot which they had found the second day of their arrival in the Land of the Giants.

"Well, it's over now," yawned Barry, patting the excited Chipper. "Gee, I'm tired."

"Well, that's a novelty," laughed Valerie, helping Barry to his feet. "You should go on a train ride every day then perhaps we wouldn't have our usual trouble in getting you to bed.

Steve edged his way out of the cab door along the ridge of metal above the churning, thundering wheels.

But after that little adventure, I should think just about everybody is ready to turn in!"

Steve glanced across at Dan. He had been sitting nursing his cup and staring into space for a full five minutes.

"What's wrong, Dan?"

The co-pilot shook himself from his reverie.

"I was just wondering whether we might have enjoyed ourselves with the old man. He seemed a kindly sort of guy—and he meant us no harm."

"There's more to it than that, Dan," Steve cut in, sensing the other man's sadness. "What's really troubling you?"

"Well, don't laugh, but as a young boy I always wanted to be an engine driver. Today, I nearly had a childhood dream come true!"

Walking down a country lane, a farmer was surprised to come across a sign which read:

LAND FOR SALE
DIRT CHEAP

HE'S A LAD

"I'M GONNA BUY MY DAD A WIG! IT'S DISGUSTIN' 'AVIN'A FIFTY-YEAR-OLD **SKINHEAD** IN THE FAMILY!"

KRACKPOT KWIZZ

WHAT WAS THE LARGEST MOUNTAIN ON EARTH BEFORE EVEREST WAS DISCOVERED

answer: **EVEREST!**

I'M SUFFERING TERRIBLY FROM PINS AND NEEDLES!

Young Jimmy's mother was furious when her son was stung for the third time by one of the man-next-door's bees.

"That's the third time this week your bees have escaped from the hive and stung my Jimmy! I want to know what you're going to do about it!" The man thought for a moment and then said, "Well if you like to point to the bee responsible, ma'am, I'll gladly wring its neck!"

A motorist putting his old banger into the local garage for an oil-change, received some frank advice from a mechanic.
"If I were you, sir, I'd forget the oil and change the car!"

Two smartly dressed 'men about town' bumped into each other in the street and began discussing clothes.
"Is that an Easter tie you're wearing, Charles?" asked one of them.
"No!" replied Charles. "What made you think that?"
"Because it has egg on it, old boy!" quipped the other.

MIRTHFUL MARRIAGE

A handsome boy octopus married a pretty girl octopus and they walked down the aisle, hand in hand, hand in hand, hand in hand, hand in hand, hand in hand, hand in hand, hand in hand and hand in hand!

STAN AND DELIVER

The Sun God Sets

Angry waves crashed across the strange craft's bows, scattered in a fury of foam and fell back into the sea. Time and time again they lashed at the foundering boat as it struggled desperately to keep the might of the Atlantic at bay.

It was the little craft's first day out on an incredible voyage. But, inevitably, the heavy sea took its toll. The twin steering oars were smashed, and waves cracked the make-shift repairs.

For the small, diverse crew it was an ill-start to a trip that already had amassed its own legion of doubters. The boat, setting out from Safi, Morocco, in North Africa, was intended to cross the Atlantic. But one factor made this one of the strangest journeys ever undertaken.

The boat was made of *paper!*

To the skipper, Norwegian Thor Heyerdahl, battling the seas was nothing new. In 1947 this scientist-adventurer had made world headline news by crossing the Pacific Ocean in his balsa-wood raft *Kon Tiki*. This had proved that the Polynesians might have originally drifted, by wind and current, across the ocean in rafts from South America.

Now the year was 1969 and he was out to prove another theory—that the Egyptians could have crossed the Atlantic *twenty-five centuries* before Columbus! Historians had noted a marked resemblance between the civilizations of the Mexican Mayas, the Incas of Peru and the Egyptian Pharoahs—including boats made of reeds.

So, following ancient Egyptian drawings, Heyerdahl built his boat made entirely of papyrus. He called it *Ra* after the sun god of Egypt.

The boat, fifty feet in length, weighed twelve tons and was constructed by binding papyrus reeds into bundles which were then lashed together. When completed, *Ra* looked strange indeed with its curved bows and stern. Then enough provisions for three months were stowed aboard; such things as honey, bread, olives, livestock and drinking water. This done Heyerdahl—together with his crew of six—set sail . . .

But after the setback on the first day, the Norwegian learnt that the boat had been loaded incorrectly. Consequently *Ra* had been listing and shipping water.

However, disaster finally struck fifty-six days after *Ra* had set sail. Originally, while copying the design of the early Egyptian craft, the *Ra*'s builders had come across indication of a rope leading from the top of the stern curvature to the deck. They concluded after much thought that it served no other purpose than mere decoration.

They were *wrong!*

Heyerdahl and his crew found that the rope would have acted like a bowstring and held the papyrus in

Ra puts to sea off the Moroccan port of Safi, on May 25th.

Sail

●●●●●●●●●

shape. Without it, *Ra* slowly became waterlogged and gradually began to sink.

The last moments came when success was almost in sight. Six-hundred miles off Barbados, the sea claimed the boat of paper and Heyerdahl was forced to radio for help. A storm had battered continually at the boat to act as the final death-stroke, and sharks had prevented repairs being made.

Thus, *Ra* was never to reach its destination—the Yucatan peninsula. But, nevertheless, it had proved something, at least—that it was capable of carrying seven men across two-thousand-seven-hundred miles of pounding seas!

Carpenters at work building the papyrus boat.

The construction site for the *Ra* was set against the background of the Pyramids of El-Gizah, some miles from Cairo.

FORWARD from the BACK-STREETS

GOOD LUCK, VAL. THE UNDER-23 TEAM SELECTORS ARE WATCHING THE GAME! KEEP THAT TEMPER UNDER CONTROL!

THANKS FOR THE TIP, MR. DEXTER!

VAL HUDSON, AN ORPHAN FROM GLASGOW, CAME SOUTH AND JOINED KINGSDOWN UNITED F.C. BECAUSE OF HIS HARD UPBRINGING, VAL WAS A TOUGH NUT WITH A QUICK TEMPER — WHICH OFTEN GOT HIM INTO TROUBLE...

KINGSDOWN UNITED WERE DRAWN AT HOME IN THE FIRST ROUND OF THE F.A. CUP TO WATERFORD ALBION, SECOND DIVISION LEADERS...

KINGSDOWN FOR THE CUP...

WAAATER-FORD!

ALMOST IMMEDIATELY AFTER KINGSDOWN KICKED OFF...

OOUCH!

ALL RIGHT — CUT THAT OUT! I'M NOT STANDING FOR ANY ROUGH STUFF!

WHAT DO YOU MEAN, ROUGH STUFF? I DIDN'T EVEN HAVE THE BALL. HE JUST KICKED ME!

SORRY, SON — MY FAULT!

THE WATERFORD DEFENDER SHADOWED VAL EVERYWHERE...

HEY! THAT WAS A FOUL!

HE'S PLAYING VAL, NOT THE BALL, EVERY TIME!

21

AND THEN — KINGSDOWN WERE THROUGH...

KINGSDOWN FOR THE CUP!

HURRAH!

MIGHT AS WELL SEE WHO THE LUCKY ONES ARE...

AFTERWARDS, AS VAL WAS WALKING HOME...

FANCY GETTING MY NAME TAKEN — WITH THE SELECTORS WATCHING AS WELL! THAT RUINS **MY** CHANCES!

CLASSIFIED RESULTS! UNDER-23 SIDE NAMED!

SPORTS

HOT-HEAD HUDSON BOOKED!

BUT CHOSEN FOR UNDER-23 GAME

Val Hudson, fiery-tempered Kingsdown striker, scored two goals this afternoon but had his name taken. Later the selectors picked Hudson for the Scottish Under-23 team to play the Italian Under-23 side in Milan, next week . . .

HOT-HEAD HUDSON! THEY'RE MAKING ME OUT A RIGHT VILLAIN! STILL — I'M IN THE INTERNATIONAL! MUST BE MY LUCKY DAY!

ON MONDAY MORNING...

CONGRATULATIONS, VAL! I KNEW THEY COULDN'T LEAVE YOU OUT!

THANKS, MR. DEXTER! WE'RE FLYING TO MILAN THIS AFTERNOON!

SOON, THE SCOTTISH UNDER-23 TEAM, INCLUDING VAL, WAS ON ITS WAY...

WELL, LADS, WE'VE NO TIME TO LOSE ON THIS TRIP. WE'VE ONLY ONE DAY FOR PRACTICE BEFORE THE GAME...

DINNA WORRY, BOSS — YE'VE GOT THE BEST SIDE YE'VE HAD IN YEARS!

IN MILAN THEY WERE LOANED A GROUND FOR PRACTICE...

FIVE-A-SIDE FOR HALF AN HOUR, LADS! PLAY IT HARD — VAL, KEEP THAT TEMPER UNDER CONTROL!

WELCOME TO ITALY, MR. BALFOUR. DO YOU MIND IF I WATCH — FOR THE NEWSPAPERS...?

HELLO, RENALDI — SURE HELP YOURSELF — YOU'LL SEE WHAT YOUR BOYS ARE UP AGAINST TOMORROW!

I'M-A SURPRISED YOU FELT YOU HAD TO WARN YOUR PLAYER HUDSON ABOUT LOSING HIS TEMPER!

OCH, AWA', MON — THAT WAS A JOKE! THE LAD HAS SPIRIT— BUT HE'S NO' A DIRTY PLAYER!

THE SESSION ENDED...

OKAY, LADS — THAT'S ENOUGH. YE SEEM TO BE WORKING WELL TOGETHER. TAKE A SHOWER — THEN BACK TO THE HOTEL FOR AN EARLY NIGHT!

LATER, AT THE HOTEL...

SEEN THIS PAPER, VAL? THE ITALIANS SEEM TO HAVE IT IN FOR YOU!

I DON'T UNDERSTAND ITALIAN — READ IT OUT, TOM!

IT HAS A BIG HEADLINE—'MANAGER WARNS HUDSON TO CONTROL TEMPER'! IT GOES ON TO SAY GINO GRETTI IS THE SURPRISE CHOICE TO PLAY AT CENTRE-HALF — SPECIALLY TO MARK YOU!

I KNOW THIS GRETTI. HE'S A BIG, ROUGH, TOUGH PLAYER. HE'LL GIVE YOU PLENTY OF TROUBLE, VAL!

THE BIGGER THEY ARE, THE HARDER THEY FALL. I'M NOT BOTHERED, SIR!

WEDNESDAY AFTERNOON — FIVE MINUTES TO THREE — AND THE SCOTTISH UNDER-23s RAN OUT BEFORE A MASSIVE CROWD...

GOOD LUCK, LADS. SWING THE BALL ABOUT — AND SHOOT HARD!

VAL RAN TO RETRIEVE ONE OF THE PRACTICE BALLS...

BOOO!

IT'S ALL THAT TOUGH STUFF THEY WROTE IN THE PAPERS — THE CROWD IS AGAINST ME BEFORE THE GAME STARTS!

TAKE NO NOTICE, VAL — THEY'RE ONLY TRYING TO NEEDLE YOU!

I KNOW — BUT IT MAKES LIFE TOUGH, THOUGH!

AS SOON AS THE GAME STARTED, GINO GRETTI AND VAL CLASHED...

UUGH!

OUCH!

IT WAS VAL WHO CAME OFF BEST...

WHAT'S UP WITH 'EM? I DIDN'T FOUL HIM!

FORGET IT, VAL — JUST DON'T PAY ANY ATTENTION!

BOOO!

BUT EVERY TIME VAL RECEIVED THE BALL...

BOOOO!

IT'S ALL RIGHT BEING TOLD TO 'FORGET IT' — BUT I CAN'T! WHY PICK ON ME, ANYWAY?

AT HALF-TIME...

THEY'VE GOT EIGHT MEN BACK — THEY'RE PLAYING FOR A DRAW. MOVE FASTER — YOU'VE GOT TO CRACK THAT DEFENCE!

MY LEGS ARE BLACK AND BLUE!

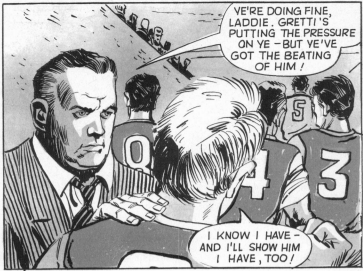

YE'RE DOING FINE, LADDIE. GRETTI'S PUTTING THE PRESSURE ON YE — BUT YE'VE GOT THE BEATING OF HIM!

I KNOW I HAVE — AND I'LL SHOW HIM I HAVE, TOO!

AGAIN AND AGAIN GRETTI BOWLED VAL OVER...

LADDIE — USE THIS SPONGE — IT'LL FRESHEN YE!

I'M OKAY — AND I'LL SHOW THAT BLOKE WHAT'S WHAT! I'VE HAD ENOUGH!

FIVE MINUTES FROM THE END OF THE GAME — THE ITALIAN DEFENCE CRACKED WIDE OPEN...

HE'S A-BEATEN GRETTI — HE'S THROUGH!

INCREDIBLY, VAL DID NOT SHOOT...

WHAT'S UP, CHUM? YOU'RE LOSING YOUR GRIP — YOU DIDN'T FOUL ME!

THE SCOTSMAN — HE'S-A MAD! HE'S TAKING THE BALL BACK TO GRETTI!

HE COULD HAVE WALKED IT INTO THE NET! WHY HE GO BACK?

An artist's impression of the first lunar jeep
to be used as a means of moon travel.

Inflated tyres are no use on the moon. All lunar rovers will have
some form of flexible wheel. This one is made of wire mesh.

Lunar crew to Mission Control: "All systems checked out. Ready to descend. Speed 5 miles per hour. She kicks a bit but we can handle her. Heading straight for bottom of crater."

Mission Control: "Roger. Don't get lost. And watch out for those lunar traffic cops."

The light-hearted banter between the astronauts and their ground controllers means that the mission is going well.

But the astronauts have already landed on the moon. Now they've embarked on *another* pioneering venture. They're bouncing along in their *lunar rover*—a kind of electrically-driven, lightweight lunar jeep. The target, a mile or so away, is a large crater. They will plunge over the rim and hold tight as their versatile little runabout jolts to the bottom.

The Americans have had a busy time since Neil Armstrong made the first historic footprint on the moon and said the most quoted words in the annals of space flight: "It's one small step for a man, but a giant leap for mankind." With flights to the moon on a regular schedule, the missions have become more adventurous, the astronauts more confident. More ambitious experiments have been set up on the lunar surface. Bigger quantities of moon rocks have been brought back to earth for analysis.

But, until now, the astronauts have had to stay within walking distance of their lunar landing craft. That is why the Apollo 17 mission is so important. The American astronauts have, for the first time, a vehicle to roam around in. The exploration of the moon can really start.

In contrast to some of the more way-out designs for lunar surface vehicles, the first lunar rover looks refreshingly familiar—almost like an Earthbound jeep, in fact.

It is a collapsible buggy which will carry two astronauts, their hand tools and other equipment, and has room for large consignments of rock samples.

Separate motors drive each of the jeep's wire mesh wheels, which have metal treads to give the vehicle traction

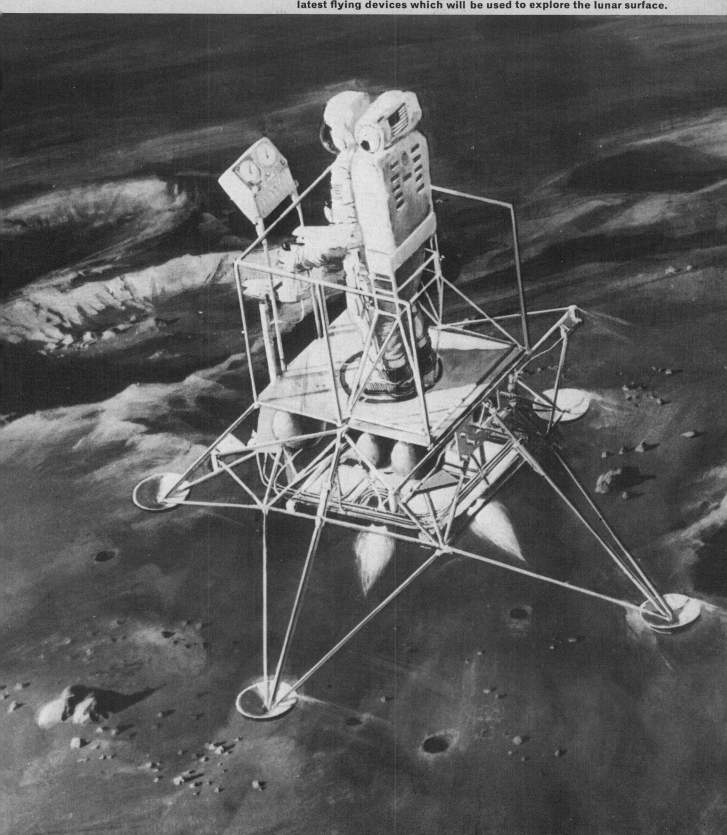

The Fleep – Flying Excursion Experimental Platform – is one of the latest flying devices which will be used to explore the lunar surface.

on the dusty surface. Each motor is operated independently, so that a power failure on one wheel won't affect any of the others. Power is supplied by chemical batteries that can be recharged on the moon. Speed is up to 10 miles-an-hour.

The plan for Apollo 17 is to make up to four trips in the area around a large crater called Tycho, which is situated in rugged highland territory near the moon's equator. Tycho was formed by the explosive impact of a meteor, which seared about 200 feet into the moon, throwing up rock from an area deep below the surface.

By collecting samples from the crater, the astronauts should be able to bring back for scientific study a cross-section of the top 100 feet or so of the moon's crust. As one space official put it: "That's like letting nature do your drilling for you."

The first lunar rover has been deliberately kept small, and has been built largely of lightweight aluminium, so that it can be carried safely inside the Apollo spacecraft. Fully loaded with crew and equipment it weighs just over 900 Earth lbs., but only 150 lbs. in the low gravity conditions of the moon. It will travel to the moon in the storage bay of the lunar module which is being modified to make space for it.

Later, more roomy landing craft will be available, and with them bigger and more advanced lunar roving vehicles. These will be of two types, wheeled vehicles which can carry both men and equipment, and one- or two-men

The rocket-belt, being tested above, will enable astronauts to take long strides on the moon.

Jet-propelled boots are another method of taking giant steps on the moon.

flying machines known as 'Fleeps'.

All the rovers which travel on the moon's surface will have to be built to overcome the big problem posed by the moon's gravity. The weak gravitational pull of the moon—only one-sixth as strong as the Earth's—makes it difficult for wheels to grip on the surface. Inflatable tyres like those used on cars aren't much good. Pressure inside them would make them explode. Nor is plastic or rubber likely to stand up to the extreme temperatures of the lunar day and night, though for very short expeditions lasting only a fraction of the long lunar day (equal to 14 Earth days) a heat-resistant form of these materials might be possible.

In general, however, the wheels of lunar rovers will be made of metal and be flexible so as to adjust to the bumpy surface. Each wheel will have the suspension built right into it, again to prevent nauseating and dangerous bouncing, and each wheel will be driven by its own electric motor.

Several vehicles like this are under development and a few have already been tested. On Earth, of course.

One of them, appropriately called *Explorer*, is used in the field training of astronauts. This can be done quite realistically on volcanic lava fields in Arizona, which are not dissimilar to the rock-strewn surface of the moon.

Besides being able to cope with very rough surfaces, a lunar rover should ideally require a minimum of effort by the driver. So *Explorer* is equipped with simple stick controls, both at the front and at the rear. This means that manoeuvring is fairly simple, even for an operator wearing a pressurized space suit.

For use on Earth, *Explorer* is fitted with a petrol engine and massive solid rubber tyres. When it goes to the moon it will have fuel cells to provide power and flexible wheels. Cruising speed will be 15 miles-an-hour, with a top speed of about twice that much.

A more advanced concept of lunar rovers is the *Molab*, which is both a house and a means of transport for lunar explorers. Astronauts will be able to operate inside *Molab* for up to 14 days and cover distances of up to 300 miles.

Several different types of *Molab* have been proposed by different aerospace firms. Each would carry a crew of two and about 600–700 lbs. of scientific equipment; including machinery for deep drilling. The fuel cell power system would provide drinking water as a by-product and a small store of dehydrated food would be carried aboard.

Other features of the *Molab* finally approved for lunar exploration are likely to include a large forward-viewing port, television cameras for scanning the moon's surface, a pressurized cabin that would enable the astronauts to operate in a comfortable shirtsleeve atmosphere, and an airlock which would be used when they went outside.

One *Molab* prototype is fitted with a Walking Beam Suspension unit consisting of eight individually-powered wheels attached in pairs to individually-powered pivoted beams. The wheels can be raised or lowered and the beams rotated, locked or freed in any combination. By this unique system, the vehicle will be able to climb over obstacles four feet high and cross safely over crevasses seven feet wide!

For covering really long distances on the moon's surface, the favoured method on future missions is likely to be a one or two-man personal flying vehicle.

The latest of these is known as *Fleep* —short for Flying Lunar Excursion Experimental Platform—which is propelled by rocket jets and lands on saucer-shaped feet not unlike those of the Apollo lunar landing vehicle.

Fleep is the most sophisticated of a series of personal flying vehicles, developed for use on the moon, but with potential uses on Earth as well. These include jet-propelled shoes, the rocket belt, the rocket flying chair and the rocket pogo stick. With further development they could well lead to the realization of man's ancient dream of being able to fly through the air with the ease of birds.

The rocket belt was first developed nearly ten years ago. It has since proved its reliability in thousands of tests in many parts of the world. It is strapped on to the waist, and controlled by motor-cycle type hand grips. The rocket belt has a fine burst of speed—up to 80 m.p.h.—but can at present be used only for very short journeys. Its range is less than a mile.

In the rocket flying chair the operator sits on a seat fitted over the propulsion unit. The control handles reach over his shoulders to his hands, and the vehicle is steered by movements of both the arms and the shoulders.

The flying pogo stick, a stand-up

Experts give the space taxi a trial flight. This ultra-modern means of lunar transport could be useful if astronauts ever became stranded on the moon's surface and had to be rescued.

version of the flying chair, comes in one- and two-man models. Both models can carry up to 150 lbs. of equipment in addition to their operators.

All these vehicles would be very easy to use on the moon. The rough and hazardous surface would present no obstacle, apart from landing. And, as

the flying vehicles are powered by small rockets using jets of hydrogen peroxide or a similar fuel, no atmosphere is needed to keep them aloft.

Personal flying vehicles are very expensive to develop and to run. But they will obviously play a big part in any large-scale exploration of the moon attempted in the coming decade.

TV TWENTY-FUN

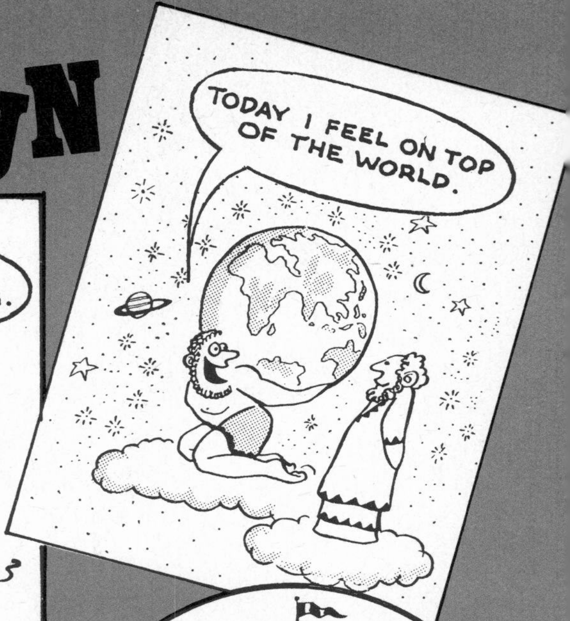

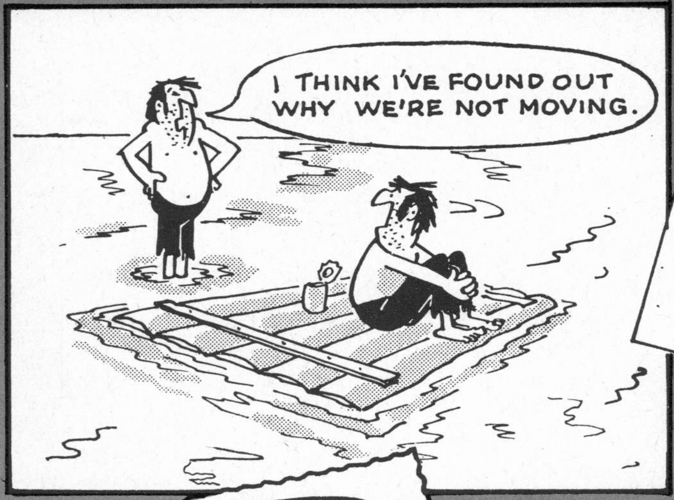

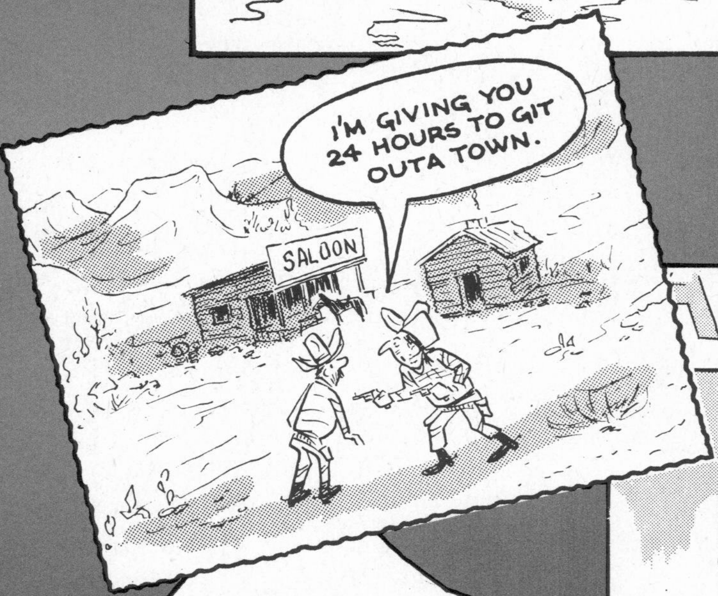

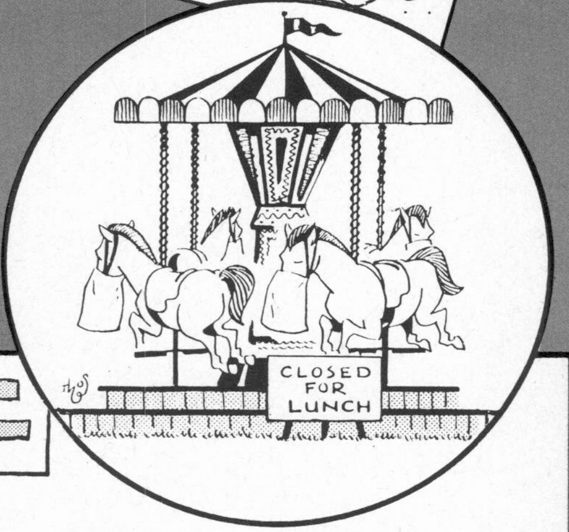

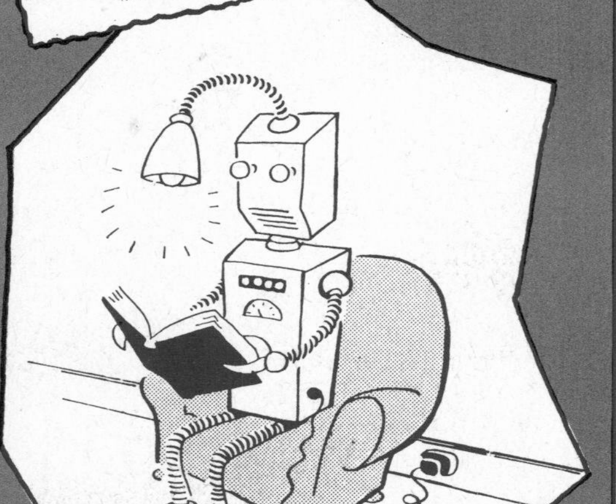

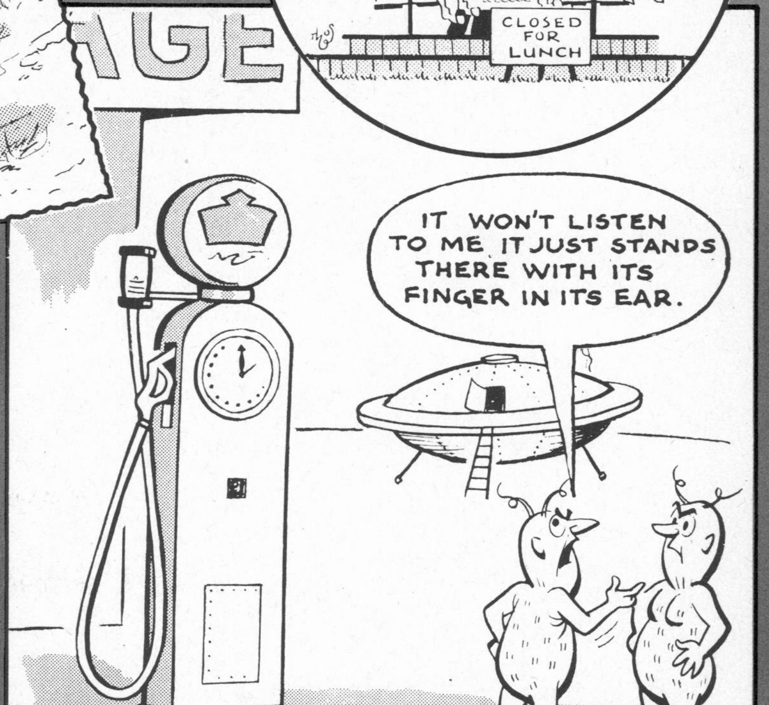

LAND of the GIANTS
Soldiers of DOOM!

THE SOUNDS OF A FAMILY ON A WEEKEND PICNIC CARRIED CLEARLY INTO THE FOREST. BUT THE FAMILY WERE GIANTS — IMMENSELY BIGGER THAN THE TINY SURVIVORS OF THE CRASHED EARTHSHIP, 'SPENDTHRIFT', WHO WATCHED, HIDDEN NEARBY...

COULD BE THERE'S SOMETHING IN THE WAY OF FOOD FOR US THERE!

FOR THE CAPTAIN OF THE MAROONED SPACESHIP, HIS CREW AND PASSENGERS, SURVIVAL WAS A CONSTANT STRUGGLE ON THE HOSTILE PLANET. BUT, THEN...

FORGET THE FOOD, STEVE! LOOK AT THAT STOVE — IT'S RUNNING ON SOLAR CELLS! WE COULD ADAPT THEM TO REPOWER OUR SHIP'S DEAD ENGINES!

IT MEANT RISKS — **BIG** RISKS — BUT ANY CHANCE OF GETTING AWAY FROM THE LAND OF THE GIANTS WAS WORTH TAKING...

DAN, BARRY — COME WITH ME. MARK, YOU STAY HERE IN CASE ANYTHING GOES WRONG!

OKAY, SKIPPER! GOOD LUCK!

AS THE CAR DOORS BANGED SHUT AND THE ENGINE COUGHED TO LIFE, MARK SPRINTED FORWARD...

AT LEAST I CAN GO ALONG AND CHECK ON THE ROUTE! I'LL JUST HAVE TO PLAY IT BY EAR!

THE JOURNEY LASTED AN HOUR AND AT LAST THE CAR PULLED UP IN A QUIET, RESIDENTIAL SUBURB...

UNPACK THE GEAR WILL YOU, MERVIN!

AW, HECK, POP! I WANNA GO PLAY!

YOU DO AS YOUR FATHER TELLS YOU!

GRUMBLING, THE BOY MOVED TO OBEY — BUT AS HE OPENED THE CAR BOOT...

WHAT...?

DON'T! QUIET, KID! GIVE US A BREAK!

OH, BOY! I'VE READ ABOUT YOU FREAKS! HOW DID YOU GET IN HERE?

NEVER MIND! IT WAS AN ACCIDENT! JUST LET US GO, HUH?

BUT MERVIN HAD OTHER IDEAS...

ARE YOU KIDDING? I'M GONNA HAVE FUN WITH YOU — AN' YOU'D BETTER PLAY ALONG, OR I'LL TURN YOU IN!

WHAT A FIND! JUST WAIT UNTIL I'VE UNLOADED THE CAR!

THERE'S THE STUFF, MA! I'M JUST GOING UP TO MY ROOM!

OKAY, SON. KEEP OUT OF THE WAY AND DON'T DISTURB YOUR PA!

37

SKY GIANT!

A single-seater jet is dwarfed by the Jumbo Jet's massive size as it flies alongside.

magine a whale in a tank of tadpoles.

Or Buckingham Palace in an estate of bungalows.

Got the picture?

Good—now you'll have some idea of how the Jumbo Jet compares with other airliners.

Jumbo—or to give it its correct (and much duller) name, the Boeing 747 Superjet—is the first of a new breed of giant airliners that will one day change our lives. Because of the huge number of passengers carried on each plane, fares for flying in the Jumbo will become lower and lower—meaning that one day we will all be able to fly wherever and whenever we want to!

LET'S GO JUMBO-JETTING!

It's a fantastic prospect, all right—but why wait? Imagine we're booked for tomorrow's Jumbo flight to New York!

"Will passengers for Pan American Flight 8090 please assemble at Gate Five," the voice blares impersonally from the loudspeakers in London Airport's spacious departure lounge. Grabbing our hand-cases and quickly finishing our coffee we hurry across to Gate Five.

Funny—there seems to be an awful lot of people here for one plane—must be four or five hundred . . .

Soon we're jogging across the tarmac in the special airport bus. Peering through the rain-splattered windows we see VC10s and Boeing 727s manoeuvring busily around and a DC9 thundering down the runway, nose-wheels pawing at the air. Big aircraft all of them. Surely the Jumbo Jet can't be *that* much bigger? Well, we'll soon know.

The bus halts by the plane and out we get. Then we stop, staring, hardly believing our eyes. Sixty-three feet high, Jumbo towers above us like a five-storey block of flats. It is two-hundred feet wide and not far short of one hundred yards long. It is *vast!*

An elevator the length of one in an underground station takes us up to the cabin door, high, high above. The air hostess welcomes us aboard. Air hostess? 'Usherette' would be a better word, for the cavernous passenger cabin is more like a cinema than the inside of an aeroplane!

Instead of the usual two rows of seats with an aisle running down the middle, there are no less than nine wide seats fitted across the width of the cabin. The photograph shows how two walk-ways separate the seats— at each side and in the middle.

We manage to grab a side seat,

looking out across the wide silver wings through reinforced windows shaped like TV screens.

"Fasten your safety belts, please," call the hostesses, and the sound pitch of the motors changes from whistle to scream.

Surrounded by twinkling dials in the cockpit high above, the captain lets his *sky giant* roll off down the runway, watching the smooth tarmac slip past nearly *twenty yards* below.

Down to the end of the long runway. Stop. Turn around. Build up the power. Release the brakes. Off we go! Fast drinking up fuel from the 50,000-gallon tanks, the four powerful Pratt and Whitney turbofan engines hurl our 7,000-ton weight down the runway. Within seconds the sixteen tractor-sized wheels lift clear and slot into their wing recesses. We are airborne!

Up, up, up we go. Finally the engine roar fades and the part of the cabin in front drops down to our own level. We have reached our cruising height and are headed towards New York at a whispering 625 m.p.h. Four and a bit hours of flying left. Nothing to see out of the windows but fleecy white clouds. This could be boring . . .

But hold on! What's this? A pretty hostess stops before us, pushing a heated trolley simply groaning under the weight of food. Soup, tender chicken, crisp green salad, the choice is ours . . .

We wade through the delicious meal, and by the time the coffee stage is reached, nearly five hundred miles have slipped by. Closing our eyes, we lean comfortably back, thinking of a man called Charles Lindberg, the first person ever to fly the Atlantic alone.

Not for him the luxury of Jumbo-jetting! Strapped in his brave little aeroplane, 'Spirit of St. Louis', flying in the darkness scant inches above the pounding Atlantic swell, never knowing if he would reach the other side and nearly freezing to death in the meantime—would he have ever believed that just forty years later huge aircraft would be roaring from one side to the other dozens of times a day?

Let's stretch our legs—there's enough room to take a dog for a walk on the Jumbo! After visiting one of the large washrooms we take a look at the luxury lounge upstairs. *Upstairs?* Yes —Jumbo is a two-storey aeroplane, with the lounge and flight deck reached via a modern spiral staircase at the front of the passenger cabin. Then, back downstairs again to stretch out in our seat to watch a good Western film. (Jumbo is a fully-equipped

cinema as well as a long-range aircraft!)

Another good meal and then the front of the cabin is tilting down— we've started the long run-in to New York's Kennedy International Airport.

The undercarriage extends out with that click and a thump that always makes us wonder what's dropped off, the hostesses call out "Please fasten your safety belts" and minutes later we're down, cruising along the runway at a slow 100 m.p.h.

In the last five-and-a-half hours we've had two good meals, been for a walk, watched an exciting film—and flown 3,000 miles.

WHY JUMBO JETS?

More and more people are flying every day. There will be three times the number of people using aircraft in 1975 than there were in 1965—and ten times the amount of cargo being flown.

Every airline in the world is competing to attract the custom of passengers. The best way of doing this is to undercut everyone else on fares. And the *only* way of cutting down on fares is to have bigger aircraft—for the more people you fly at once, the cheaper it becomes to fly each one of them. Hence, Jumbo Jets mean lower fares —and maybe Jumbo-sized holiday journeys for you!

A hostess offers a selection of foods from a trolley as passengers settle comfortably in the *nine-across* seats of the passenger cabin.

Big 'brother' Jumbo beside one of its smaller counterparts, the Boeing 727.

IF YOU ARE RIGHT, N'KEBE, I SWEAR THIS MAN-KILLER SHALL MEET TARZAN'S JUSTICE. STAY HERE IN PEACE UNTIL I RETURN.

GRIMLY, TARZAN SET OUT FOR THE TERRITORY THE PYGMIES HAD LEFT. SWORDBEAK, THE HAWK-EAGLE, BROUGHT NEWS...

LORD OF THE JUNGLE, THERE IS A LEOPARD CALLED GELFANG. HE HAS HEARD YOU HUNT HIM — NOW HE HUNTS **YOU**!

SO BE IT! SUCH NEWS IS OF HELP. CUNNING MUST MEET CUNNING, O FRIEND!

GELFANG, KING OF LEOPARDS, WAS DEADLY AND SILENT. THREE NIGHTS LATER...

NOT EVEN TARZAN CAN HUNT ME AND STILL LIVE! I AM MERCIFUL — SO DEATH SHALL BE SWIFT...

AS GELFANG LEAPT...

GRAAAAWW!

CLICK!

THE NET TRAP WORKED WITH LIGHTNING EFFICIENCY...

O GELFANG, YOU GROW CARELESS! I AM NOT SO EASY TO SLAY AS THE PYGMIES...

I SLEW NO ONE! YOU SPEAK LIES!

TARZAN, WHO COULD JUDGE MAN AND BEAST, SOON LEARNED THAT GELFANG SPOKE THE TRUTH. THE GIANT LEOPARD WAS FREED...

COME, LET US INSPECT N'KEBE'S VILLAGE. YOU, AS KING, CAN TELL ME WHICH LEOPARD BROUGHT DEATH...

I AGREE! I OWE YOU MY LIFE.

THE ABANDONED VILLAGE WAS REACHED...

THE TRACKS ARE THOSE OF LEOPARDS, GELFANG!

YET THE SCENT IS WRONG! NO FOLLOWERS OF MINE HAVE BEEN HERE.

IT IS STRANGE! LISTEN, I HAVE A PLAN, O KING OF LEOPARDS. WILL YOU PLAY YOUR PART?

SPEAK ON! I TOO HAVE A CODE.

ALONE TARZAN FOLLOWED THE LEOPARD TRACKS...

THE TRACKS LEAD THERE. IT'LL BE SAFER TO ENTER IN MY OWN WAY...

DANGER! DANGER! TARZAN!

HE CLIMBED DIZZILY...

I SMELL SMOKE! NO LEOPARD STAYS WILLINGLY NEAR FIRE...

WITHIN THE WEIRD RUIN...

BROTHERS OF THE LEOPARD CULT, WE CARRY DEATH AND TERROR LIKE TRUE BEASTS OF THE JUNGLE...

OKOH! EVERY VILLAGE WILL BE OURS.

LEOPARD-MEN! HUMAN CURS WHO LIVE BY EVIL AND KILLING...

A WILD CRY SET ECHOES A-THROBBING!

AYEE-OOOO!

IT'S TARZAN! ...KILL! KILL!

TARZAN'S CRY WAS ANSWERED...

TARZAN NEEDS US.

WE ARE READY, O GELFANG!

MEANWHILE...

I UUÜRGH!

I'M NOT KILLED YET— JACKAL!

THE ATTACKERS FROZE IN HORROR...

LEOPARDS! SUKA — DEATH! WE ARE DOOMED!

GRR.

GRRRR

GRRRR...

TARZAN CALLED COMMANDINGLY...

GELFANG, KEEP YOUR HUNTERS BACK! O LEOPARD MEN, DISARM— OR DIE SWIFTLY!

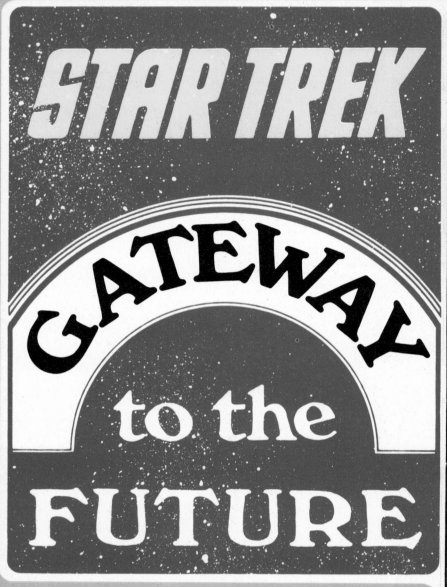

STAR TREK
GATEWAY to the FUTURE

F ar from the centre of Galaxy M-674, the dying sun grew colder, its planets slowly being pulled in . . . in towards the old star. According to calculations taken by Mr. Spock, the sun would cease to exist within fifty years and the seven planets ten years before that.

Watching the feeble efforts of the sun to shoot warmth across its solar space, Captain James Kirk felt strangely sad. He knew the universe created and destroyed stars by the hundreds of thousands. As one died, another was born in a blaze of flaming gas. Yet, it was always sad seeing the end of something so majestic as a solar system.

He thought how it would be when the Earth's sun reached this same stage—and it would, some day. All stars burned themselves out eventually. But when that time came, mankind would no longer be on Earth. He would have travelled to other star systems and settled on strange, far-flung planets across countless galactic empires.

That was part of his job—exploring space; searching the many galaxies for future homes; places man could colonise.

The second part was making peace with alien races. If man was

to voyage to other worlds he had to mix peacefully with his neighbours in space; strange neighbours—sometimes, *warlike* neighbours. . .

"Captain—look at this!"

Kirk swung from the viewport and went to Mr. Spock's side. He studied the sensor readings, the computer tapes in Spock's hands. "What is it?" he asked softly.

"I'm not sure," Spock replied. "But it looks like a life form on the fourth planet."

Kirk frowned. It couldn't be! Nothing could live on that cold, barren world. Its atmosphere had drained off centuries ago—when the sun started growing old. Even as he looked at the monitor screens, he could see that the surface was a solid sheet of ice.

"Prepare a landing party, Mr. Spock," Kirk ordered then. "Have them equipped for extreme cold." He started to swing away but then halted. "I think I'll come with you, too," he added.

Thirty minutes later, four men materialised on the weird planet's surface. Teleportation had solved many problems for 'Enterprise's' crew. With it, men could be de-materialised and 'shot' from the giant starship to a celestial body within seconds—regardless of whether or not the planet had an atmosphere capable of sustaining winged flight. That was important in space exploration. So many alien planets did not have an atmosphere above them. So many, too, were continually circled by flying hunks of jagged space junk.

Kirk stared through his visor, seeing nothing but ice around him—ice and monstrous mountains in the distance. Speaking into his suit radio, he asked: "What is your reading now, Spock?"

Spock scanned the surface with his portable sensor. Suddenly, he stiffened and snapped; "Over there, Captain—behind that near range of mountains!"

Kirk pointed with a thickly gloved hand. "Let's go, men. It's a long walk. . ."

The old man appeared as if by magic, his clothes reflecting the flashing lights from the two strange columns.

Darkness was thickening when the party reached its destination. Ahead of them, twin columns rose into the semi-blackness of the solar void. They seemed as though they might have been fashioned by man—*or a race capable of building like man*.

Kirk was reminded of those ancient pillars in Greece—the ones belonging to the wonderful temples standing above Athens. They were high—at least forty feet tall. Down the inside of each column, a series of flashing lights kept racing up and down . . . up and down . . . winking and blinking with monotonous regularity.

"What is it, Captain?" asked Crewman Shafer incredulously.

Kirk shook his head. He was about to say he didn't know either. About to say—and then he saw the old, bent figure of a man appear as if by magic.

Spock shouted: "Captain. . ."

Kirk silenced him with a curt: "I see him!"

The Earthmen watched in silence now as the old man shuffled forward until he stood between the twin columns. His tattered robes reflected the flashing lights, his furrowed face showed his unbelievable age. In one gnarled hand he held a staff—but this, like the pillars, glowed from within.

"Welcome, Earthlings," the quavering voice said. "I am the Guardian of the Future. I have waited a long time for you. . ."

Kirk was puzzled. The man spoke perfect English and he could hear him, although his suit-microphone was *not* tuned in for an outside pick-up. A quick glance at his companions showed him that they, too, were hearing that old, crackling voice.

"You are puzzled," the Guardian chuckled. "Don't be afraid. I speak in your mind—telepathically. . ."

Spock grinned. He was able to send—and receive—telepathic messages, too. His father had been a Vulcanite, his mother an Earthwoman. That was why he was different from the other crewmen of the 'Enterprise'. He, alone, was incapable of human emotions, although he could fully understand the emotions that guided his fellow spacemen.

"Why have you waited for *us*?" Spock asked in thought.

"Ah," came the Guardian's reply.

"The one called Spock is able to communicate with me telepathically. . ."

Kirk heard a soft sigh then from the old man. He didn't know what Spock had asked but he felt sure it would get them the answers they wanted to hear. He was right. . .

The Guardian waved his staff, beckoned them forward. "Come through the Gateway with me," he said. "My time is running out. I must show you the future before I depart. . ."

One of the crewmen stepped forward. Kirk barked: "Stop!" He stared at the old man: "What will *happen* to us?"

"Nothing—if you obey my instructions," came the Guardian's reply. He waved his staff at the flashing lights on the twin columns. "Centuries ago, my people discovered how to walk into the future. These lights are the Gateway. When you pass through them you immediately select a time far in advance of your own."

"A time-machine . . ." Crewman Hurst exclaimed.

"Yes," the old Guardian said with a wrinkled smile. He looked at Kirk: "And what do you wish to know about the future, Captain?"

Kirk grinned too. The old man looked exactly like the pictures of Father Time he had seen as a boy back on Earth. He trusted the other now. "I would like to see what will happen on Earth when we return from our voyages," he said.

"That shall be arranged," the Guardian told him. "Step through the Gateway. You *won't* be needing that!" he added, pointing to Kirk's helmet.

"How do we get back?" Kirk asked.

"Call me in your mind," the old man explained. "I shall know and return you to this planet."

Kirk nodded. "Spock—you come with me. You two"—and he looked at each man through his visor—"stay here! If anything goes wrong, get back to the ship and carry on without me."

Hurst slammed a gloved fist into his other palm. "I could go with you, sir. . ."

Kirk shook his head. "No, Hurst. Spock and I go—and that's final!" He motioned to Spock and, together, the two men approached the Gateway, removing their helmets and oxya-packs as they stepped between the pillars. . .

Then, as the flashing lights raced over them, Kirk felt a strange tingling in his muscles. Everything began to fade and he felt himself fall . . . fall . . .

They were in America . . . Los Angeles. Kirk recognised the freeway as it soared over Hollywood. Not far away, the Hollywood Bowl sat empty, lifeless under a canopy of twinkling stars. Sleek, radar-guided cars streaked along the express lane towards the Mexican border as others went in the opposite direction bound for Canada and the Alaskan oilfields. Local traffic scooted back and forth on the service lanes, shuttled off the controlled freeway as their destinations were reached.

"Nothing's changed," Spock remarked.

"No? Look over there . . ." Kirk said grimly.

From where they stood to one side of the freeway, they could see the military installation facing the Hollywood limits of Los Angeles. Grim-faced soldiers guarded the one, massive blaster aimed at the downtown heart of the city.

Overhead, several rockets zoomed back and forth across the valley, diving and circling areas where orange-red flashes zipped upwards at the sky.

"It's . . . it's unbelievable," Kirk muttered. His gaze swung to include a group of young people scrambling up the scrub slope near them. He could see the gleaming weapons in their hands, the grubby clothes they wore.

Within seconds, they were surrounded, phasers aimed at them, weary faces watching their every movement.

"I'm Captain Kirk of the USS 'Enterprise'," Kirk said.

A young man laughed savagely. "'*Enterprise*' foundered last week."

Kirk stiffened. If this was the future he didn't wish to know more. This wasn't the Earth he'd left. What had happened and was

Spock jabbed the 'fire' button of his phaser and the youth collapsed suddenly.

'Enterprise' really destined to be destroyed?

"Who are you?" Spock asked.

"Arrowists," the young man replied proudly.

Arrowists! Kirk knew that name. Before 'Enterprise' had departed on her voyage of exploration, the Arrowists had been peaceful hippies. They had used the name 'Arrowists' because it reminded them of the Red Indian and how he

hunted in peace with his bow and arrow *before* Columbus arrived in America.

"But," Kirk said, "Arrowists don't believe in using phasers..."

"We didn't," the other replied. "Not until the military tried to wipe us out."

Kirk exchanged a horrified look with Spock. *The military!* Had Earth been taken over by a dictatorship? Had all the years of peace

been thrown away again?

"We're from the USS 'Enterprise'," Kirk began again. "We've been exploring space for five years. What is happening here?"

The youth seemed puzzled. "Don't you honestly know?"

"Would I ask if I did?" Kirk snarled.

Turning to his grim-faced companions, the youth said: "I think he's telling the truth. *But,* the radio said 'Enterprise' had been destroyed by an asteroid bombardment as it passed near Mars!" He seemed lost, wanting to believe Kirk yet mystified by what he had heard.

Kirk grinned. "I can't explain how we happened to be here but, please, trust us. We have no part in your fight. We just want to know what's happening on Earth."

"Look," the youth said, pointing to the military installation across the freeway. "See how they keep their weapons aimed at the city? That blaster they have built can fire only once. But should it do so —at *us*—then there would be need for nothing more. See how *ready* they are to fire on everything that moves against them? Perhaps, one day, they *will* even use the blaster."

Kirk could see the weapons— and the soldiers crouched behind them. "I see," he said slowly.

"A year ago," the long-haired youth explained, "we were willing to accept a new ruling that all Arrowists kept to restricted areas. We were willing to suffer hardships and primitive conditions just so we could continue to live as we wanted. But even that wasn't enough for the military. They demanded we surrender our bows and arrows and beg for what little food they decided we must have to exist upon."

Spock nodded, speaking now. "You refused and started fighting."

"Yes," the youth said. "We fought. We fought and fought until now there are only a few thousand of us left."

"How many of you were there before the fighting?" Kirk asked.

"Fifty thousand!"

Spock grinned. "Ten thousand," he said calmly, reading the youth's mind.

Kirk shook his head in wonderment. Even if there had been ten thousand, that meant almost nine

thousand had been wiped out!

Spock raised his phaser-transceiver and asked: "Mind if I call our ship?"

The youth bristled. His eyes widened and his face tensed. "No! *Don't!*"

"Why?" Spock asked with a smile.

"We . . . we . . . ," the youth stammered.

Spock turned the phaser until it aimed at the youth. He jabbed the 'fire' button and the youth collapsed suddenly. Before the others had a chance to use their own weapons, Spock swept them with the deadly phaser—coldly smiling as each fell to the ground.

"Spock!" Kirk shouted.

"It's on *stun*," Spock explained as the last Arrowist slumped forward.

"You'd better have a good reason for this," Kirk warned.

"I have," the super-intelligent Spock replied. Bending over the youth, he went through the other's pockets. Then, holding a slip of paper, he straightened, reading the scrawled words written on it. "Long live Arrowists! Anybody else is an *enemy*!"

Kirk glared across the freeway to the military post. "And that means?" he asked the unemotional Spock.

"I can tell you *when* we capture that installation," Spock laughed. "You see, Captain—there is something you forget. We entered the Gateway of the Future. But how *far* into the future did we travel?"

Kirk looked at him questioningly.

Spock smiled, then explained: "Have we actually returned to Earth?"

"Certainly," Kirk said. "This is Los Angeles..."

"Is it?" Spock asked and, without warning, started running for the freeway...

Almost as soon as Spock dived into the fortified installation, Kirk realised that the soldiers were aliens . . . extra-terrestials. He recognised the insignia attached to their shoulder-flashes, the long faces. It seemed like years ago when the 'Enterprise' had ventured into Nobian territory...

Kirk's fists windmilled, clobbering soldier after soldier. Phasers were useless against Nobians. He could see Spock chopping—rabbit-punching man after man—sometimes pausing to land an uppercut to an alien jaw as he charged through the emplacement.

Experience had taught Kirk a hard lesson. He avoided Nobian fingers reaching for him. He knew that the aliens' fingertips gave off an electrical discharge equal to a thunderbolt. It would take just one touch at the nape of a human neck.

He reached the Nobian weapon, the massive blaster which overpowered all the smaller, surrounding weapons, and swung the barrel. Aiming at the barren hillside, directly behind the Hollywood Bowl, he fired. The crackling energy bolt disintegrated the hillside, in one searing blast.

"Behind you . . ." Spock's voice yelled.

Kirk swung, landed a perfect hook to the alien's jaw. All about him, Nobian soldiers lay sprawled in defeat.

"Glad you fired the blaster," Spock said then, grinning, and dusting off his clothes.

Kirk laughed softly. "We could not take the chance of having Los Angeles. . ." He stopped and asked: *"Is it Los Angeles?"*

"No!" Spock replied. "We've landed after Earth perished when our solar system's sun burnt out. The 'Enterprise' the Arrowists spoke about is probably another starship mankind sent out centuries *after* us."

"Where is this then?" Kirk asked.

"I don't know," Spock answered. "But wherever it is—we've changed the future! Rest assured—mankind will leave Earth. But when he does somebody will come along to save him from the aliens."

Kirk smiled, thought about his own time—his return to the Gateway. . .

The old, bent Guardian laughed softly as Kirk and Spock materialised between the flashing columns. "Did you have an enjoyable visit?"

Kirk smiled. "Yes, we did! Thanks, old man—we can make a

record now for our descendants to follow."

"I'm glad," the old man said. "I was worried. You see—somebody *had* to know what could be. Had to warn the others. . ."

"Our children?" Kirk asked.

The old man nodded, started to vanish. For a second his body shimmered into brilliance. Then, quickly, it faded—faded as his thought-voice said: "The stars are not always constant, Captain. Nor is mankind's future. With your knowledge, your Earth-people can be saved from a terrible fate. Make sure you write all that you have

seen into the records. One day, another Captain Kirk in another USS 'Enterprise' will value your report. That way, Earthmen will always be here to help other civilisations to find their way. . . ."

The voice ended, and the Gateway lights blinked for the last time. Now, the twin columns were just columns—stone carved by some forgotten hand. The future had been revealed. It all depended on Captain James Kirk—of the USS 'Enterprise'. Or perhaps another Captain James Kirk—of another USS 'Enterprise'. . .

Kirk raced for the massive blaster as, behind him, Spock lashed out savagely.

I'VE GOT A SP⚽RTS-MAD DAD!

THE SAINT MEETS THE MIND-MASTERS

THERE WERE THREE THINGS THAT SIMON TEMPLAR – ALIAS THE SAINT – COULD NOT RESIST: A PRETTY FACE, A CHALLENGE AND AN APPEAL FOR HELP FROM AN OLD FRIEND. IT WAS THE LAST OF THESE THAT WAS TAKING HIM ALONG A NARROW LANE IN THE WILDS OF CORNWALL, WHEN SUDDENLY...

OF ALL THE BLITHERING IDIOTS! HE'S BACKING STRAIGHT INTO ME!

SIMON'S SWIFT REACTIONS SAVED HIM. THEN...

SAY, PAL, IT'S ABOUT TIME YOU WORE GLASSES!

WHO DO YOU THINK YOU'RE...?

I MUST APOLOGIZE. WE ARE BIRD-WATCHERS! WE HAD JUST SEEN A RARE SPECIMEN, AND I'M AFRAID WE WEREN'T THINKING!

HAPPIER FOR THE APOLOGY, SIMON DROVE ON. IT WAS NOT LONG BEFORE HE REACHED HIS DESTINATION...

I'D LIKE TO SEE PROFESSOR HUMPHRIES. MY NAME IS SIMON TEMPLAR!

GOVERNMENT RESEARCH CENTRE

JUST ONE MOMENT, SIR. I'LL PHONE THROUGH!

BUT INSTEAD OF PROFESSOR HUMPHRIES...

WELL, IF IT ISN'T CHIEF INSPECTOR CLAUD EUSTACE TEAL OF SCOTLAND YARD. WHAT BRINGS YOU TO CORNWALL?

I MIGHT ASK THE SAME THING OF YOU!

SIMPLE, MY DEAR CLAUD. I'M JUST VISITING AN OLD PAL, PETER HUMPHRIES!

H'MM! I DON'T LIKE IT! BUT I SUPPOSE I CAN'T STOP YOU. ALL RIGHT, YOU CAN GO IN!

54

A FEW MINUTES LATER...

YOU SOUNDED PRETTY WORRIED ON THE PHONE, PETER. SUPPOSE YOU TELL ME WHAT ALL THE TROUBLE'S ABOUT?

IN A NUTSHELL, SIMON, I'M SCARED OF BEING KIDNAPPED!

TWO OTHER SCIENTISTS AND MYSELF ARE WORKING ON THE PLANS OF A NEW TANK. THE PROTOTYPE HAS ALREADY BEEN BUILT. FOR SECURITY REASONS EACH OF US ONLY DEALT WITH A SECTION OF THE BLUEPRINT – A THIRD EACH!

THE OTHER TWO SCIENTISTS HAVE DISAPPEARED. THEY SIMPLY WALKED OUT OF HERE IN THE MIDDLE OF THE DAY – AND VANISHED. I COULD BE NEXT...

SO THAT'S WHY TEAL AND HIS BLOODHOUNDS ARE DOWN HERE!

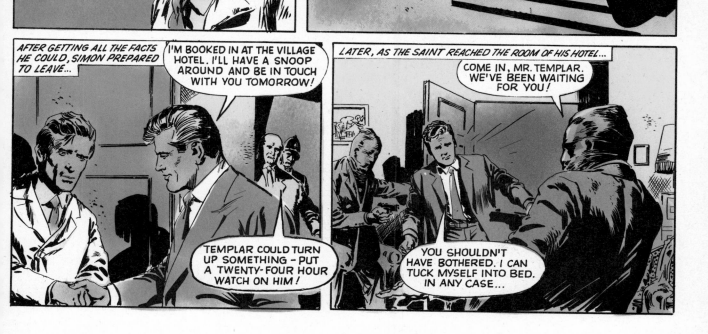

AFTER GETTING ALL THE FACTS HE COULD, SIMON PREPARED TO LEAVE...

I'M BOOKED IN AT THE VILLAGE HOTEL. I'LL HAVE A SNOOP AROUND AND BE IN TOUCH WITH YOU TOMORROW!

TEMPLAR COULD TURN UP SOMETHING – PUT A TWENTY-FOUR HOUR WATCH ON HIM!

LATER, AS THE SAINT REACHED THE ROOM OF HIS HOTEL...

COME IN, MR. TEMPLAR. WE'VE BEEN WAITING FOR YOU!

YOU SHOULDN'T HAVE BOTHERED. I CAN TUCK MYSELF INTO BED. IN ANY CASE...

UNFORTUNATELY, SIMON DID NOT HAVE EYES IN THE BACK OF HIS HEAD...

HALF AN HOUR PASSED. THEN...

SIMON, ARE YOU ALL RIGHT? WHAT...?

OF COURSE HE'S ALL RIGHT, PROFESSOR. AND SO WILL YOU BE IF YOU DO AS YOU'RE TOLD!

FORTUNATELY, THE SAINT WAS NOT THE ONLY ONE THAT TEAL HAD BEEN WATCHING...

LOOK OUT, TEAL!

PHEEEP!

WHAT THE DEUCE...?

THAT WHISTLE WILL BRING EVERY COP IN THE VILLAGE - EVEN IF THE GUN-SHOT WON'T! LET'S GET OUT FAST - AND BRING THE MACHINE WITH YOU!

THE THREE MEN DISAPPEARED INTO THE NIGHT. AFTER ORDERING A SEARCH PARTY, INSPECTOR TEAL RETURNED...

ALL RIGHT, TEMPLAR. LET'S HEAR YOU TALK YOUR WAY OUT OF THIS!

THE MEN HAVE TAKEN THE HYPNOTIZING MACHINE WITH THEM. TEAL WON'T BELIEVE A WORD I SAY... HELLO, THAT LIGHT...

THE REFLECTION IN THE WINDOW GAVE SIMON THE CHANCE HE WAS LOOKING FOR...

I HOPE THAT LORRY OUTSIDE HAS A SOFT TOP!

PHEW! MY LUCK'S IN!

MOMENTS LATER SIMON, TOO, DISAPPEARED INTO THE DARKNESS...

NEXT MORNING, A GROCERY VAN ARRIVED AT THE RESEARCH CENTRE...

WHERE DO I TAKE THESE GROCERIES, CHUM? THE REGULAR CHAP'S ILL! THIS IS MY FIRST VISIT HERE!

THE COOKHOUSE IS THE THIRD BLOCK ON THE RIGHT. YOU CAN'T MISS IT!

ONCE INSIDE THE CENTRE, THE ELDERLY VAN DRIVER MADE STRAIGHT FOR PROFESSOR HUMPHRIE'S ROOM...

PETER, IT'S ME! I'LL EXPLAIN EVERYTHING LATER – BUT FIRST IT'S VITAL YOU SHOW ME WHERE THE OTHER TWO SCIENTISTS WORKED!

I... TEAL TOLD ME TO INFORM HIM IF I SAW YOU. OH, HECK! IF I CAN'T TRUST YOU WHO CAN I TRUST? COME ON!

THIS IS ONE ROOM. THE OTHER ONE'S NEXT DOOR!

I KNEW IT! AND THAT MUST BE THE TANK BELOW. LISTEN, PETER, I WANT YOU TO ...

THE SAINT WHIRLED AS THE DOOR OPENED...

I HAD AN IDEA YOU'D RETURN, TEMPLAR. I'M ARRESTING YOU ON SUSPICION OF KIDNAPPING AND ESPIONAGE!

THAT'S WHAT YOU THINK, CLAUD!

SEEMS I SPEND ALL MY TIME JUMPING OUT OF WINDOWS. HOPE THE STUNT MEN'S UNION DOESN'T GET TO HEAR ABOUT IT!

GUARD, STOP THAT MAN!

SORRY, CHUM— BUT THE TANK'S MY ONE CHANCE. I'M GAMBLING THAT I CAN MANAGE THE CONTROLS!

UUUH!

THE SAINT WAS IN NO MOOD TO BE STOPPED...

LET'S HOPE MY THEORY'S RIGHT— OTHERWISE I'M REALLY FOR THE HIGH-JUMP!

ON THE EDGE OF THE WOOD, NEARBY...

IT'S TEMPLAR! HE MUST HAVE SPOTTED US! LET'S MOVE OUT OF HERE— AND FAST!

THE SAINT HAD HIS OWN IDEAS ABOUT THAT...

BOOM!

I THOUGHT THOSE PHONEY BIRD-WATCHERS WOULD BE HERE— AND THEY'RE STAYING!

AS I THOUGHT! THE CAR CONTAINS A LARGER VERSION OF THE HYPNOTIZING MACHINE— WHICH CAN SHINE STRAIGHT INTO THE TWO SCIENTISTS' ROOMS FROM HERE!

BUT FOR YOU, TEMPLAR, WE'D HAVE HAD HUMPHRIES, TOO. HE WAS BOUND TO HAVE ENTERED ONE OF THOSE ROOMS SOMETIME!

IT WAS NOT LONG BEFORE INSPECTOR TEAL ARRIVED...

AH, CLAUD! SO GLAD YOU COULD COME! IF YOU ASK OUR FRIENDS NICELY THEY'LL TELL YOU WHERE THE SCIENTISTS THEY KIDNAPPED ARE HIDDEN AWAY!

IF THEY DON'T SEEM VERY TALKATIVE— JUST REMIND THEM WHAT AN ITCHY TRIGGER FINGER I'VE GOT!

THE TUNNEL!

Denver—capital of the American state of Colorado—is like all other cities the world over; a metropolis of thriving industry, busy streets and even busier highways. But beneath the crowded streets lay another world—one of silence and eternal darkness. It was this world that Ted Calloway was returning to. . .

Due to a car accident, he had been in hospital for three years and had spent a fourth convalescing. Now he was ready to resume work. But Ted's job was no ordinary one—not for him an office and desk. His work-tools were a helmet and torch; his workplace, the labyrinth of winding sewers and storm-drains that weaved beneath ground.

There was not an inch of the large maze of tunnels that he had not studied. But during his absence nobody had taken his place, and now Ted had to make a general survey.

So, dressed in a plastic overall, helmet and mask, he descended into the darkness, his torch beam throwing a piercing finger of light before him.

His eyes soon became accustomed to the familiar ill-lit surroundings his torch picked out. Ahead, lay the entire length of silent, lifeless tunnels.

Passing along the major 'avenues', he inspected the smaller ones, making mental notes of any necessary repairs. Finally, he reached one of the tunnels under the older part of the city. So far, Ted had continued occupied by his own thoughts, and the working routine which he knew inside out, even after four years. But now, strangely, he hesitated. Somehow—for some inexplicable reason—he felt uneasy. His torch-beam darted lithely about. Everything seemed in order . . .

Then he checked, as his memory came back. He had grown used to seeing the many rats scurrying about —in fact, almost accepted their

presence willingly as the only other form of life he would encounter. But now there were none to be seen!

With his torch he inspected the big cracks in the walls. Nothing. He shrugged his shoulders and continued, telling himself the uncertainty he felt was solely his imagination. After all, he had been away for a long time.

He continued his inspection until he reached the darkest and lowest corner of one of the tunnels. The intense silence seemed almost to envelop him, pressing hard on his ears. Then again came that slight feeling of alarm.

Ted started to walk forward, his head craning eagerly. It was at that moment, that he halted in mid-step . . . Behind him came a savage roar which echoed incredibly down the full tunnel length. For a moment, Ted could hardly breathe, every muscle in his

body numbed. Then, slowly, he turned and shone his torch in the direction from which the weird sound had come.

At first the light settled only upon the familiar tunnel wall. But perhaps it was because Ted Calloway was afraid to shine it anywhere else . . .

Gradually, he eased the beam around, struggling to make his blanched, tense hand respond. It was then that he saw the silhouetted outline. Ted stared—as though hypnotized—into the cold, baleful eyes that observed him. It was impossible, he told himself. But, a slight movement proved otherwise.

Just five or six feet away, stood a fully-grown *alligator!* Its jaws slightly open to reveal the line of needle-sharp teeth, the huge creature edged forward. Momentarily Ted remained motionless, struggling to prevent himself from panicking. In those brief few seconds, a whirl of questions raced across his mind.

Where had the alligator come from? What should he do . . .?

But his own instinct answered the last of those for him. Spinning round, he ran back along the tunnel, the torch beam throwing an erratic light.

Ted was surprised to hear his own voice crying out. His one thought was of the massive creature that he could hear scuffling after him. Tunnel followed tunnel, twisting and curving in an endless maze.

Suddenly, a searing pain brought his senses reeling back. Nursing his bruised cheekbone, he glanced up at the iron pole which he had struck lightly, projecting from the wall.

But, later, Ted was to thank that 'lucky' blow. It had calmed his panic, brought back his reason.

He turned. Yes, already he could hear the strange scuffling noise again growing increasingly louder. The alligator was hunting him.

But now Ted was ready. Swiftly, he

summed up what he should do. He did *know* the tunnels. Of course, that was it! A manhole! All he had to do was climb up one of the many manholes, into the sun-drenched street.

But even as the thought occurred to him, so did another. He had run frantically, without thinking. Now, he was in a blind alley from which there was no escape. *He was trapped!*

Once again, he held his breath, remaining quite still as he listened to the sound of the approaching creature. He could hear its strange breathing. Then came the noise of its feet . . .

Next moment, the massive alligator was standing hesitantly at the entrance to the tunnel. Almost instinctively, Ted swung his torch so the beam settled directly upon the reptile's snout. Ted knew it would be the last movement he would ever make . . .

But he was mistaken!

The piercing light held the alligator transfixed as it shone brilliantly into its eyes. Ted cursed himself for not having realized before. The creature had grown accustomed to the darkness and the powerful torchlight obviously blinded it! Then Ted took his one chance. Slowly, he edged towards the alligator, keeping the torch directed upon the creature's savage face. With every step, he expected the alligator to suddenly lunge forward. He felt beads of perspiration running down his forehead. But he didn't dare lift his hand to wipe his brow.

Ted glanced briefly over the creature towards the ledge behind it. Then he tensed, drew a shallow breath and jumped. In a fraction of a second he was down again, landing safely behind the creature. He began running once more. But this time he knew where he was heading. . .

There was a dull thud as the manhole cover fell back and Ted pulled himself thankfully up into the daylight—and *safety*. A few startled passers-by looked at him strangely, but their faces hardly registered the amazement that the police did when Ted hurriedly blurted out his fantastic story.

That same evening, a group of men returned with him to capture the alligator, using the same method that had worked so well to stun the creature before. By shining a light directly into the reptile's eyes, it was an easy task to slip a strong net over its scaly body.

Later, it was transported to the local

zoo and its story soon made it a star attraction. People flocked to see it and to murmur incredibly between themselves.

How had the alligator managed to become trapped in the first place? That was the question which baffled Ted Calloway, police and authorities alike. But, eventually, the truth came to light . . .

A family had taken a holiday in Florida, some years earlier. While there, they had visited the famous Everglades, an extensive area of marshland where wildlife abounded. The father had agreed to buy his son and daughter a baby alligator which had just hatched from its egg. Both brother and sister were delighted and the family returned to their home in Denver.

It was some little while later that the creature disappeared. In fact, it had been washed away down a sluice pipe —only to reappear, a fully-grown alligator—the day Ted Calloway discovered it in . . . *the tunnel!*

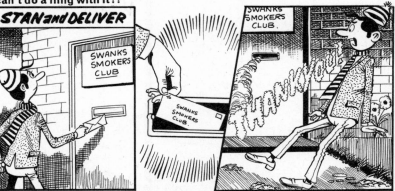

SPACECROSS

Got your pen ready? Then countdown to this crossword to carry you across space and back to Earth again!

CLUES ACROSS

1. Spacemen and oilmen—this American city is famous for both (7) ✓
4. First one up—and the Russians called their spacecraft a . . . . (7) ✓
8. Beyond the Earth's atmosphere (5) ✓
10. It is emitted from the sun (5)
12. Scandinavian god of thunder (4) ✓
14. Periods of time (4) ✓
16. Weapons used by Star Trek crew (7) ✓
18. Human-like machines (6)
20. Heavenly body which revolves round the sun (6)
22. Goddess of Love and is also 20 across (5)
24. Sloping letter, in short (4)
25. National Aeronautics and Space Administration (4) ✓
26. Sorrowful (3)
27. Help (3)
28. To plan a space course, for example (4)
30. Mischievous children (4)
33. Egg-shapes (5)
36. Type of bird (6) ✓
38. Secret agents; they could be spies (6) ✓
39. You're not underhand if you bowl like this (7)
40. Obtain by merit (4)
42. You'll skid if it bursts (4) ✓
43. Made of oak (5)
45. Used for tracking spacecraft, for example (5) ✓
46. Mission . . . . , an astronaut might say this (7)
47. The hottest part of the hottest place in the Universe (7)

CLUES DOWN

2. Union of Soviet Socialist Republics (4)
3. North-north-east (3) ✓
4. The sun (3) ✓
5. Observe (4) ✓
6. It has ten moons (6) ✓
7. Astronauts might make these to other worlds (6)
9. Mountains separating France and Italy (4) ✓
11. To catch your breath (4)
13. Revolution around the earth, for example (5)
15. 6 down has these (5)
17. Male child of a parent (3)
19. The TV satellite was meant to startle (anagram) (7)
21. Touching down or . . . . (7)
22 & 32 down. A piece of apparatus in a spaceship which gives pictures (5–6)
23. Celestial bodies appearing as luminous points in the sky (5)
29. Of the moon (5)
31. English coin of low value (5)
32. See 22 down.
34. It surrounds the earth (3)
35. Respect (6)
37. Centre of an egg (4)
38. In the middle of (4)
41. Midday (4)
42. Journey (4)
44. Nothing (3)
45. Royal Yacht Squadron (3) ✓

Solution on page 77.

ASSIGNMENT SUB-ZERO!

The squat and ugly shadow of the transport plane dances across the ice at 120 m.p.h. Bigger and bigger it grows as the needle in the Hercules' cockpit swings steadily towards zero. 100 feet . . . 50 . . . 25. . .

The dark profile flashed over the perimeter fence on to the runway. Scant feet above, the practised eye of the American pilot scans lazily over the glowing instruments.

Then he lets the big 'bird' down. . .

A brief scream of undercarriage hitting ice, the sudden roar of four jet props on reverse thrust, and shadow · and plane merge into one.

Exactly nine hours, forty minutes before, we took off from Christchurch, New Zealand. The weather was warm there; far too warm for the Polar Outfits the air force men had insisted we wear. These consisted of thermal underwear, then layer after layer of wool, fur and cotton and gigantic insulated boots.

We were also issued with bright-orange rubber suits. "If the pilot has to ditch in the ocean you might be able to last forty minutes wear-

ing these," the man had comforted. We grinned bravely. Forty minutes didn't seem so long to us.

The Antarctic Circle was far behind us when the coast of the great sub-continent came into view. How grim and inhospitable it looked! Far below we could just pick out the shimmering white surface of the Ross Ice Shelf, a floating glacier the size of Western Europe; then the smoky peak of

Mount Erebus, a dying volcano named after a British ship of exploration in 1841. How startling the black volcanic ash around the summit is – like a great blot of ink on a snowy-white exercise book. But there is no time to stare – for in its shadow lies our destination; the blue, green and orange buildings of McMurdo, America's number one base in Antarctica.

McMurdo is a sort of Cincinnati

Antarctica covers an area of 6,000,000 square miles. You can follow the course of the U.S. ice-breaker, 'Atka' which, in January, 1955, reconnoitred the Ross Sea area, to select the site for a U.S. base.

During the Byrd expedition to the Antarctic, weather balloons were released to determine wind direction.

This strange, bowl-shaped piece of apparatus is one of seven attached to a jeep-like vehicle called a 'weasel' (five at the front and two at the back). By emitting electronic currents, the device is capable of detecting hidden faults in the ice.

A scientist uses an instrument called a hand auger to remove an ice sample for inspection.

of the South Pole – everything is done to remind the American personnel of life back home in the States.

But today the thermometer registers 18 degrees Fahrenheit, a near heatwave for McMurdo. Although the clock reads midnight, the sun shines down from a cloudless sky. It is daylight and will remain so for another four months. And then the night will descend on Antarctica for the whole of the winter.

Down here, winter is a dreadful experience. The temperature can sink to an incredible *minus* 127 degrees Fahrenheit in some places and the wind whips along at about 185 m.p.h. Storms break at a

moment's notice and in the white hell of a South Pole snowstorm the visibility drops to nothing; you can't see your feet and you can't stand up anyway!

The most evil-weathered place in the whole of Antarctica is Byrd, about 650 miles from the South Pole itself. The U.S. headquarters at Byrd is built underground, out of the way of the howling, freezing climate.

Only ventilation pipes, emergency exits and observation platforms brave the surface plus, of course, an American flag, its stars and stripes tattered and shredded. It takes a real emergency to get a man 'upstairs' when the weather gets bad!

Although the Americans have poured more money into exploring this grim place than any other nation, Antarctica belongs to every country in the world. There are no frontiers and we are all free to send our scientists on peaceful missions of research and exploration.

Weapons are banned; American and Russian, Czech and Briton, men of many nations work side by side, bound together by a common thirst for knowledge.

But what a paradise Antarctica is for students of wild life! Ten million seals and many times that number of penguins live and die on the 'White Continent', protected by the fact that the whole of Antarctica is a nature reserve.

Two scientists make their way down the entrance hatch to the radio research laboratory built under the snow at New Byrd Station, Antarctica.

Scientists examine the interior of a hut at Cape Royds, set up by Sir Ernest Shackleton, a British explorer in 1908–9. Many of the provisions left here are still in good condition after over half a century! That's deep-freeze for you!

As there are no natural markers in a snow field to guide a plough operator, this target sled is used to ensure a straight path is cut.

Plants and fauna exist just as they have done for millions of years, untouched by the heavy boot of civilization. Creatures of land, sea and air show no fear of man. They come close, curious but not afraid. They have no memories of a huntsman's rifle . . .

The South Pole! To stand here is to feel the ultimate achievement. This is truly the end of the earth – the southernmost point of our planet as it spins through the universe. Whichever way you look you're looking due north. Extraordinary! This is also the point where the International Date Lines converge; you can pass from Today into Tomorrow and back again into Yesterday, depending on whether you step left or right.

The Pole is the loneliest place on Earth. Above us is an empty sky. Below nothing but solid ice and around us nothing but a deathly-white stillness all the way to the horizon. Only in the Polar base itself is there any sign of life as the American scientists hurry from one building to another.

Life at the Pole is naturally hard but between taking samples and studying the strange atmospheric conditions the Americans try and make it as easy as possible. The camp is equipped with cinema and club-room. There is a sun-ray lamp to get a tan and the chef will even provide a birthday cake! But, nevertheless, it is the same Pole that prompted Captain Scott to write in his diary in 1912: 'Great God – what a horrible place'. It had taken Scott 80 days to drag himself and his team across the frozen wastes to be first at the Pole. 80 days of sheer freezing agony and at the end of it the only reward was the sight of the Norwegian flag left by Amundsen a bare month before. He had been beaten, and a broken man, he died there.

No. Antarctica hasn't changed. It is as cold and as horribly bleak as it always was – and when the explorers of the seventies leave their aeroplanes and their heated cabins behind them, they know it! They know that the white hell of Antarctica is their master!

SPACE SWOTS

Monday morning. It's raining. You look at your school time-table: history, geography, French . . . It's going to be one of those days you tell yourself, as you reluctantly leave the breakfast table.

◀ Once within this chamber which simulates conditions in space, a trainee undertakes various exercises which experts can then determine.

Weightlessness is one state which astronauts must experience in outer space. ▶

Astronauts check out the spacecraft during a simulated test in the Centre. ▼

Suddenly a few words from the news reporter on the radio, nearby, make you hesitate.

"The American lunar astronauts are about to leave the Apollo craft for the moon's surface . . ."

Immediately your thoughts hurtle you across space to those few chosen men, the space-capsule and an 'out-of-this-world' adventure that *you* would long to go on. Just think of it, being an *astronaut*: the blast-off, the journey through space, perhaps to some other planet, and international fame when you splash-down to earth again. Certainly a world apart from your approaching school lessons. If only YOU could be one of those astronauts . . .

But it is not as simple as you might think!

Before an astronaut even gets one foot off the ground he, too, has his own studies to follow. Taking lessons to be an astronaut might *seem* a lot more exciting than your own, but one peep into the activities of a 'space school' and you would probably be only too pleased to scuttle back to your classroom before you could utter the word *countdown*.

General training for astronauts lasts for approximately eighteen months. But, even before this starts, most candidates have 1,800 hours or more jet-fighter training under their belts.

For the first four months, three days of each week are spent within the Manned Space Centre, the other two days being reserved for field trips, which could even take the men to such places as the famous Grand Canyon in Arizona.

Not bad, you mutter enviously. But such visits are for a specific purpose—to familiarize the would-be astronauts with the best examples of landscapes that might be encountered on the moon.

Lessons within the Centre commence each morning at 8 a.m. (Probably a little earlier than you have to arrive at school!)

Immediately, the first two-hour class gets under way. Then another follows. That brings it up to lunch-time, which also lasts for a couple of hours. But, in case you are thinking that's a lot longer than *you* get, astronauts are expected to spend this break-period maintaining peak physical fitness in the gym.

But what about the lessons themselves? What sort of subjects are involved? The answer to that is *technical* ones—and plenty of them. Some of these are geology, navigation, flight mechanics, physics of the upper atmosphere and space, bioastronautics and astronomy. Just think of all that studying—might even be worse than your own, after all!

Of course, *your* school, no doubt, provides you with plenty of outdoor sports facilities. But when trainee astronauts get outside, they don't have such a comfortable or recreational time. It is nothing for them to be dropped in a desert area or dense jungle and told to reach a certain destination. It's all part of their survival training. And, even when they return indoors again, there is still no letting up. They can expect to find themselves fully immersed in a tank of water (to determine body density) or spun in a centrifuge at an incredible pace (to test reactions of the heart). Hardly pastimes to be envied!

As the training progresses, the men must go through a series of environmental courses. They use machines called *simulators* to experience exactly how to dock their space capsule, and perfect other manoeuvres which will be expected of them when actually out in space. They will also be taken up in an aircraft which makes a parabolic arc, to give them the feeling of weightlessness for a very brief time.

Finally, at the end of his course, *if*

an astronaut is accepted, he might find himself in a rocket heading for outer space. Then he dare not forget even one tiny item that he has been taught.

However, there is always the one element which he *cannot* be briefed about—*the unknown*. Man has only begun to knock at the door to the universe. And as he continues to venture deeper and deeper into it, there is no telling what he might come up against.

That is why each astronaut must be hand-picked and trained to almost super-human standards. And that means hard work—and plenty of it!

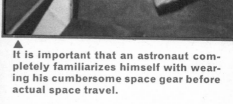

▲ It is important that an astronaut completely familiarizes himself with wearing his cumbersome space gear before actual space travel.

◀ Gemini-5 pilot, astronaut Charles Conrad, prepares for water survival tests in a Gemini space suit.

This giant centrifuge can be rotated at speeds of up to 200 miles an hour.
▼

THE GIANT MAKER

LAND OF THE GIANTS

TO THE CREW AND PASSENGERS OF THE CRASHED EARTHSHIP 'SPENDTHRIFT', THE FOREST WHERE THEY LAY HIDDEN WAS A REFUGE FROM THE HOSTILE GIANTS WHO RULED THE PLANET. A NORMAL SEARCH, EVEN WITH DOGS, WOULD NEVER HAVE FOUND THEM. BUT PROFESSOR MAGNUS KARSH WAS CONDUCTING NO *ORDINARY* SEARCH...

DEAR ME! I MUST FIND THEM — I **MUST**! MY EXPERIMENTS *DEPEND* ON IT!

IT WAS BARRY, OUT TO EXERCISE HIS DOG, CHIPPER, WHO FIRST SENSED THE PROFESSOR'S PRESENCE...

A GIANT — AND HEADING STRAIGHT FOR THE CAMP! I'D BETTER WARN THE OTHERS!

THE BOY SCUTTLED LIKE A RABBIT TO THE CLEARING WHERE THE SPACESHIP WAS CONCEALED...

CAPTAIN! EMERGENCY! AN OLD MAN — HE'S CARRYING SOMETHING...

WARN FITZHUGH AND THE OTHERS, BARRY! STAY ON GUARD TILL WE GET BACK!

D'YOU THINK WE CAN DRAW HIM OFF, STEVE?

SO I HAVE MADE A DISCOVERY – A MEANS OF TRANSFORMING MATTER! OF INCREASING IT IN SIZE! AND YOU – **YOU** SHALL BE MY GUINEA-PIGS!

BE GRATEFUL! YOU WILL BE ABLE TO LIVE **NORMALLY** ON THIS PLANET! YOU WILL BE AS WE ARE!

YAAGH!

THE GUY'S MAD! HE THINKS HE CAN **GROW** US TO HIS SIZE!

FIRST OPPORTUNITY OF ESCAPE, WE'VE GOT TO TAKE IT!

YES, BUT **THEN** WHAT? HE'LL JUST COME TO THE FOREST AND FIND US AGAIN WITH THAT GADGET OF HIS!

IT TOOK TWENTY MINUTES FOR THE PROFESSOR TO REACH HIS HOUSE, SET ON THE EXTREME EDGE OF A VILLAGE...

...A DISMALLY FURNISHED PLACE WHERE EVERY PENNY HAD GONE TO THE EQUIPPING OF ONE ROOM – THE BASEMENT LABORATORY...

NOW, MY LITTLE FRIENDS! YOU MUST BE PATIENT WHILE I MAKE READY!

NEXT MOMENT, A LID SLIPPED BACK, AND...

WH...WHAT?

LET'S GET OUT OF HERE — WE MAY BE SMALL, BUT IF THAT OUTSIZED CREATURE NOTICES US...

KARSH IS CLEAR! HE'S SLAMMED THE DOOR ON IT!

THE GAP UNDER THAT SAME DOOR WAS THEIR ESCAPE ROUTE — AND NOT A MOMENT TOO SOON...

THE SMASHED ELECTRICS IN THERE! THEY'VE SET THE LAB ON FIRE!

EVEN AS THEY REACHED THE SAFETY OF THE GARDEN...

SLOWLY, THE ECHOES OF THE BLASTING EXPLOSION DIED...

MY LIFE'S WORK! EVERYTHING — GONE!

DARNED GOOD JOB — COME ON, LET'S MAKE OUR WAY BACK TO THE FOREST. I DON'T THINK WE NEED FEAR PROFESSOR KARSH ANY MORE!

OR HIS 'DETECTOR' GADGET — THAT MUST HAVE GONE UP WITH THE REST OF HIS EQUIPMENT!

I'VE GOT A SPORTS-MAD DAD!

AH, STEP IN, SON. YOU'RE JUST IN TIME FOR A BOXING LESSON!

UH?

REMEMBER, SON, THE *FIRST THING* IN BOXING IS TO PUNCH STRAIGHT AND *HARD!*

OOOMPH!

HERE, SON! NOW YOU HAVE A GO...!

YOU BET. HERE'S WHERE I GET MY OWN BACK!

DON'T FORGET THE FIRST RULE, SON!

DON'T WORRY, POP! I WON'T!

I'M GOING TO ENJOY THIS! I'LL SHOW HIM!

BLAM!

BUT...

WHOOSH!

BOOMPH!

UUUUPHHH!

WH...WHAT HAPPENED?

I JUST DEMONSTRATED THE *SECOND* RULE, SON — *FOOTWORK!* HAVE TO KEEP LIGHT ON YOUR TOES, TOO!

LAUGH-IN

COP THIS LOT

A policeman knocked on Mrs. Brown's door, not knowing how he was going to break some tragic news to her. When Mrs. Brown appeared, he began trying to explain.

"It's my sad duty to tell you that your husband has smashed his spectacles, Mrs. Brown!"

"Smashed them?" she exclaimed. "How on earth did he manage that?"

"He was hit by a bus!" replied the policeman.

WHAT AN 'OWLER

One owl to another owl: "I feel shocking, Harold! I haven't slept a wink all day!"

KRACKPOT KWIZZ

ARE ELEPHANTS TOO BIG TO ENTER TELEPHONE KIOSKS? Answer: HOW CAN THEY BE IF THEY'RE ALWAYS MAKING TRUNK CALLS!

ANOTHER 'OWLER

Two owls hoot as they perch on a branch, being soaked by a heavy downpour of rain.

"TOO WET TO WOO!"

Two cannibals were enjoying a meal from their cooking pot.

"Your wife makes a delicious stew!" remarked one of them.

"Yes!" said the other, "I shall miss her!"

A housewife complained to the local fishmonger,

"That pound of cod you sold me yesterday wasn't half as nice as the piece I bought last week!"

"That's funny!" remarked the man, "because it was off the same fish!"

Solution to SPACECROSS (from page 64)

Across
1. Houston; 4. Sputnik; 8. Space; 10. Light; 12. Thor; 14. Eras; 16. Phasers; 18. Robots; 20. Planet; 22. Venus; 24. Ital; 25. N.A.S.A.; 26. Sad; 27. Aid; 28. Plot; 30. Imps; 33. Ovals; 36. Canary; 38. Agents; 39. Overarm; 40. Earn; 42. Tyre; 43. Oaken; 45. Radar; 46. Control; 47. Sunspot.
Down
2. U.S.S.R.; 3. N.N.E.; 4. Sol; 5. Note; 6. Saturn; 7. Visits; 9. Alps; 11. Gasp; 13. Orbit; 15. Rings; 17. Son; 19. Telstar; 21. Landing; 22. Video; 23. Stars; 29. Lunar; 31. Penny; 32. Screen; 34. Air; 35. Esteem; 37. Yolk; 38. Amid; 41. Noon; 42. Trip; 44. Nil; 45. R.Y.S.

Edgar Rice Burroughs

TARZAN and the

It was raining and had been raining for many days. The whole wide sweep of African jungle crouched dumbly beneath the blinding torrents that fell from the unseen sky. Tarzan of the apes and Lord of the Jungle, gazed from the mouth of a cave over his misty domain.

"It seems that before long, the world itself will be turned to water," he mused. "Is that your thought, too, Tika?"

The intelligent chimpanzee, holding his master's hand for comfort, looked mournfully up and nodded in dismal agreement.

On the morrow, however, Tarzan was awakened from a deep sleep by his animal friend tugging at his hair. He went to the entrance of the cave and looked forth upon a different world. The sky was blue, the sun warm and the whole jungle steamed with moisture, like a giant kettle.

"We will go downstream and visit Umtali, chief of the Kiwanis," Tarzan decided. "His tribe lives close to the river and it may be that the waters have brimmed their banks and flowed into the village. If this is so, he will need help."

He put back his head and, with both hands to his mouth, gave a trumpeting call that sailed high and clear above the smoking trees. A hoarse bellow came in answer and the bushes parted to reveal a huge elephant lumbering in response to the ape-man's command. Tarzan leaped lightly down from the cave mouth to the back of the beast, Tika following nimbly behind.

Tarzan leaned over to the huge, flapping ear and murmured one word. "Umtali!"

An hour later, the animal halted close to a full-fed river that rushed between banks that had once been steep, but now looked barely high enough to hold back the water.

Another half day of rain and there would have been a different tale to tell, Tarzan thought. But now all is well.

Suddenly, his hand sped to the knife at his belt as a black, hurtling form sprang with a rustle of leaves from an overhead tree branch!

A hard shoulder, driven by sinewy muscles and iron-hard legs, rammed Tarzan from his perch. He landed heavily on the ground, the figure on top of him. He struggled to wrench the knife from its sheath but steely fingers paralyzed his wrist in a nerve-numbing grip. The jungle lord kicked out viciously with his legs, tore his other hand free for a rocketing punch and then— burst into laughter!

Tika joined in, springing down onto the broad shoulders of the laughing black giant who bounded to his feet and gave Tarzan a hand to rise.

"Umtali!" smiled Tarzan as they clasped hands. "Is this fit welcome for an old friend?"

"I saw you coming from the village," said Umtali. "It came into my mind to test whether the Lord of the Jungle could be taken unawares by a weakling like myself."

"You are no weakling," replied Tarzan. "And I *was* taken off my guard." He indicated that Umtali should join him on the back of the elephant. When they were seated, he went on to ask: "How fare your people, Umtali? Have the rains affected them?"

"In truth, they are in better spirits now that the waters from Heaven have ceased," the native chief answered. "But they have been cooped up too long and the younger warriors grumble and are restless."

Tarzan frowned. He remembered how in the past, the Kiwanis had always been a proud and warlike race. It would be a bad thing if the warriors took it into their heads to revert to their evil ways.

"The sooner they are back at work in the fields, the better," he said serious-

ly. "Hard work is the best cure for bad thoughts . . ."

An enormous roar cut short his words. The face of the creeper-clad hill above them seemed to slide and sway. Then the ponderous mass broke out and loomed over them like a dark, falling cloud. This time Tarzan *was* on the alert. He snatched up the muscular form of Umtali as if the

As the soaked hillside slid towards them like a dark ponderous mass, Tarzan snatched Umtali and hurled himself from the elephant's back.

WINGED HEAD

chief had been a feather.

His other hand whipped around a stout vine dangling from a branch. He dived from the back of the elephant as the beast panicked and headed back towards the avalanche of mud.

Umtali felt branches whip his face, drawing blood. He crashed into the trunk of a tree as Tarzan's gigantic swing carried them clear from the black

doom. Then he was lying, dazed and winded, behind some bushes, Tarzan beside him as the lava-like landslide rolled past, four yards away, with a noise like thunder. The mountain of mud poured over the bank and into the river.

"Tika!" said Tarzan anxiously. He ran towards the hill which gaped open above them, stripped of vegetation. To

his relief, the chimpanzee, chattering with fear, came to greet him from behind a massive rock where it had taken refuge.

Suddenly, the chimpanzee shied away as a huge, flopping shape rose from the depths of the fallen cliff. What seemed like a muddy tentacle reached towards the two men. They both drew back in alarm, only to sigh with

relief as the elephant revealed itself, coated with mud, but unharmed.

"It takes more than a landslide to stop that one!" grinned Tarzan.

"*Aeeee!*" murmured Umtali softly, looking up at the huge hole. "The weight of the rain must have weakened the earth and it fell. But for you, Tarzan, it would have been a quick burial for all of us!"

"It is strange how this can happen," the jungle king said thoughtfully. "Solid ground should not be washed away like dust before the wind. Come, let us look further."

Leaving the elephant piping river water over itself, the two friends clambered up the slippery slope of the fallen cliff. But agile as they were, Tika, now recovered from his fright, scampered in front of them and disappeared into the hole.

Seconds later, a blood-curdling shriek brought both men to a halt. Tika came bolting out of the opening and sprang into his master's arms. He pointed back, chattering, and Tarzan looked puzzled.

"What nonsense is this?" he said roughly. "He tells me about men with Winged Heads in there!"

He strode towards the entrance but Tika, having suffered two bad scares in a few minutes, remained where he was. Umtali kept close behind Tarzan and almost bumped into him as he stopped suddenly. He heard his friend's quick intake of breath, and as he looked around he felt a cold shiver ripple over back.

Light filtered into the large cave and showed the remains of a mouldering table and rough wooden chairs. Crumbled almost to dust nearby lay the grinning skeletons of twelve or more men.

All around them were scattered two-handled metal swords, double-headed axes and some scraps and pieces of rusted armour. A skeleton's head rested on the table, wearing a tarnished round helmet with carved wings sprouting from either side. In one corner, stood a huge bell, a massive affair inside which a man might have crouched. Tarzan and the native chief looked at each other in awe.

"These people...skeletons," Tarzan said. "What do you know of this, Umtali?"

"The elders of our tribe once spoke of a strange, bearded race wearing these same winged helmets!" Umtali

answered. "There is an ancient legend that they came up the river from the ocean, hundreds of moons ago. They conquered our people and set them to work the mines in this district. They took a strange metal called gold from the mines and brought it back here."

"But they were a cruel and hateful race," continued the native. "The story has it that our tribe rebelled against them. My people brought down a huge landslide, entombed the invaders and burnt their ships."

Tarzan struck the bell with one hand and grunted.

"It is as heavy as an elephant," he muttered. "But I can see no sign of this gold you spoke about."

Umtali was more intent on inspecting a two-handed sword.

"Bah! I am interested in steel not gold," he said, "and this blade has still a keen cutting edge."

He swung around, sword poised as a figure darkened the cave mouth behind them. The newcomer was a short, squat young Kiwani whose name Tarzan remembered as Galazi.

"We saw the cliff collapse on top of you," he explained. "We hurried here as fast as we could and . . ." He broke off, his eyes goggling around him at the contents of the cave.

"Fear not, Galazi," laughed his chief. "They have been dust these dozen centuries, but if you are frightened of them, take a weapon to defend yourself."

He tossed a Viking sword to the warrior who caught it in one deft move-

Light filtered into the cave, revealing weapons strewn all about them and a massive bell, inside which a man might have crouched.

ment. His eyes glistened as he made the blade sing through the air.

"Tell the others to come in and choose a weapon each," said Umtali. Tarzan looked on, frowning. Was it a good thing, he wondered, to hand over these still useful weapons to young warriors, especially ones with the warlike history of the Kiwanis? Still, he reflected, it was none of his business. He kept silent but watchful as the tribesmen, forgetting their initial fear, crowded in to help themselves to the spoils of the cave.

One man rapped with his sword on the large bell.

"What is to be done with this, O chief?" he asked.

As Umtali hesitated, Tarzan broke in.

"Bring it down to the village on a wooden sledge," he suggested. "It will serve as a signal bell. When you are in trouble, sound it and the whole jungle will hear and come to your aid."

His suggestion was received with shouts of approval and soon the ponderous object was occupying pride of place in the village. Umtali looked at where it hung, slung by a heavy rope from the stoutest tree in the village. He turned to Tarzan.

"It shall hang there for ever as a token of our friendship, my brother," he announced.

"It is well," said Tarzan. "But at the moment, your brother is weary and would rest."

The two friends went off to Umtali's hut and after a frugal meal, they fell asleep, Tarzan lying in a hammock and the chief beside him on a pallet spread on the dirt floor. Some hours later, the ape-man awoke, with a light in his face and a sword at his throat!

The burning torch was held by one of Umtali's warriors and the sword by Galazi. He wore the winged Viking helmet while other natives, armed with the Danish axes, thronged the hut.

"What foolery is this?" bellowed the chief as grass ropes were wound around his writhing body.

"Silence, Umtali!" said Galazi. "Your tribe has a new chief now—me. I will make the Kiwanis as great as they were—and masters of the whole area. With these new and powerful weapons, we will overthrow the Argori and the Masani tribes and become their new rulers."

Tarzan groaned softly to himself. What he had feared, had come to pass. The new weapons had turned the heads of the young Kiwanis. But, for the moment, there was nothing he could do. Ropes were tied about him until he could move neither hand nor foot. Then the natives left to congregate in an excited group outside.

"Fools!" said Umtali bitterly. "It is as if some fever has entered into their blood."

"Then it is up to us to cure them, my friend," said Tarzan. "First, I must summon Tika."

The jungle man uttered a low, fluting call which went unnoticed in the general babble of noise. But somewhere outside someone else heard and Tarzan grinned in the darkness. It was lucky for all their sakes that Tika preferred a tree perch to retire to, instead of a hut! A moment later, they heard a furtive scratching at the roof and straw and thatch fell upon their heads.

Umtali looked up as the hole was widened and Tika's face peered in at them. The animal swung easily down and when it saw Tarzan's bonds, it began to chatter animatedly. Hastily, Tarzan cut the animal short by extending his bound hands.

"Less talk and more action!" he commanded.

Tika obeyed his master so well that within minutes, both men were free.

"What now?" Umtali asked tensely.

"Through the roof and into the jungle!" the ape-man ordered.

He knew that the rebels were not vicious men, just misguided, and he had thought of a way to bring them to their senses without putting Umtali into the position of having to fight his own tribesmen.

Ten minutes later, they were standing in a clearing, lit eerily by the moon. Tarzan uttered a peculiar, strident cry that floated out over the silent jungle. For long minutes nothing happened. Then came a rustling in the bushes and the chief cried:

"A buffalo!"

He turned smartly on his heel, intending to flee from this, the most dangerous of African animals. Instead, he found himself staring into the red-rimmed eyes of another buffalo. He turned and there was another one.

"They . . . they've surrounded us!" he stammered.

"Fear not, Umtali, they are my friends," smiled Tarzan. He slapped one of the animals on the rump affectionately. "*I* called these creatures. They are going to help us show Galazi and his men that they are not as invincible as they think."

Holding the arched horns of one animal, he swung himself astride and gestured to Umtali to do the same.

"You . . . you *are* sure they know which side they're on?" the chief asked nervously.

"Why don't you ask them and find out?" said Tarzan easily and before this unanswerable reply, the native fell silent.

With Tika riding behind Tarzan, the trio headed for the village, the buffaloes moving like wraiths in the moonlight. On the outskirts of the village, Tarzan gave his mount head and it broke into a thundering gallop, its companions following suit.

Galazi was addressing his admiring followers when he heard the din. He took one look at the charging animals and abruptly took to his heels. A burly tribesman stood his ground, axe ready for a blow at the buffalo. But Tarzan saw the danger. He dived clear over the spread horns and knocked the man sprawling in the dust.

The buffalo swerved aside, put down its head and knocked another rebel sailing through the grass wall of an empty hut. Umtali's mount slammed its massive head into a winged Viking helmet and the native who had been wearing it, fled for cover, screaming with fear.

Tarzan smiled. "It seems that the wings have left the helmet and are now on his feet!" he remarked.

He grabbed a hanging vine and swooped easily up into a tree. From this vantage point, he could keep an eye on things and make sure that no women and children came out from their huts while the battle was raging.

With Tika riding behind Tarzan, the trio headed for the village, the buffaloes moving like wraiths in the moonlight.

But already it was nearly over. Most of the tribesmen were huddled in corners and behind huts, now thoroughly cowed—except for *Galazi!*

His eyes burning with revenge, Galazi had a Viking axe poised over one shoulder, aimed at the unprotected back of Umtali. Tarzan's hand whipped around a vine and he swung in an arc through the air—but not towards the assassin. The upthrust of his swing brought him close to the huge bell and his knife flashed once in the moonlight. As the rope parted, the bell dropped.

Some sixth sense must have alerted Galazi and he glanced up. But too late. The bell engulfed him in a cast-iron prison, muffling the frightened shriek that burst from his lips.

Half an hour later, the sheepish rebels were lined up in front of their chief. Umtali began by describing them as treacherous wretches, jackals who would round on a man only if his back was turned to them.

"O feeders on dead meat!" he cried. "Look at your chief, the man you worshipped. Listen to his high and mighty commands now!"

With one of the battle axes, he struck the bell with all his might. From inside, came a muted yell of pain and protest as the reverberations rolled round the bell. Again and again, the chief hit the bell, while Tarzan stood by smiling quietly and Tika clapped his hands together in admiration.

"And this is the man who was to be your leader," Umtali said contemptuously. "Bring him forth!"

A dozen willing hands shoved the mass of metal over on to its side. Galazi was revealed, one hand to his aching head.

"Spare me! Spare me!" he wailed. "It seemed that when I picked up the winged helmet, and the sword, a change came over me. The curse seemed to tell me to rise and kill, but now it has passed and I am my own man again."

The chief's face softened. "It may well be that there is a spell in the ancient weapons," he said. "But, remember," he went on sternly, "*I* am your chief and you are subject to me. Take all these helmets, the swords and axes and drop them into the deep pool below the waterfall." Should you ever dare to defy me again neither Tarzan nor I will deal so leniently with you."

As the humbled Africans hurried to do his bidding, Tarzan strolled over to the bell. There was a small crack in it

Tarzan swung in an arc through the air . . . and his knife flashed once.

now, due to Umtali's repeated hammerings and the fall it had sustained. Then the ape-man gave an exclamation and bent forward to inspect the edges of the surface split more closely.

"It's gold!" he breathed. "The whole thing is made of gold melted and moulded into the shape of a bell and covered with just a layer of metal!"

That served to explain several things. Where the gold mined by the black slaves had vanished to and why the bell was so enormously heavy.

The Vikings must have melted down the gold into this shape when they realised they were hopelessly entombed. I suppose they decided that this way no one else would ever lay hands on it, Tarzan thought.

"Umtali," he said casually. "This bell is no longer of any use. I think it

would be as well if it went with the others."

The chief shrugged carelessly and gave his orders. An hour later, Tarzan watched as the bell toppled into the waterfall pool with a sounding splash, there to embed itself in the muddy ooze on the river bottom.

"Better for the fishes to have it," Tarzan told his chimpanzee friend. "They alone will share our secret. Human beings change when they get close to the yellow metal. Galazi sought wealth and riches by plundering from the neighbouring tribes of the Angori and Masani. But, if only he knew that he had crouched in a bell shaped of *gold!*"

SEA CITY

Dogger Bank lies twenty-five miles out in the North Sea, between the winkle-stalls of Great Yarmouth's seafront and the towering drilling-rigs of the Hewett offshore natural gas fields.

Man is fast running out of living space. Only a quarter of our planet is dry land; the rest is ocean. And our growing numbers are filling that quarter to bursting-point. We have to find a new place to live if we are to survive. There are three choices: on other planets, underground, and on the sea. The last of these seems the easiest choice.

With this in mind, the idea of Sea City has been born—and what a fantastic idea it is! The architects who have planned this amazing place have built beautiful scale models to show what they have in mind. Looking at the models, our thoughts catapult us into the future—to the day when Sea City could be a reality . . .

Right: *Clouds superimposed on a screen behind the illuminated model give a realistic impression of Sea City at dusk.*

Below: *This exact model is even equipped with miniature ships and jetties.*

The hoverferry from Great Yarmouth skims across the choppy sea and within minutes of embarking the gaunt outline of Sea City appears on the horizon. Our first impression is of a great curving concrete wall, stark and white, sweeping upwards and outwards from the grey sea. How beautiful it is—but how grim and inhospitable, too! Surely, 30,000 people can't live in a fortress like this?

But then the hoverferry reaches a gap in the wall of concrete—and we see how wrong our first impression was. Inside the egg-shaped outer wall, sixteen tiers of gleaming, glass-fronted houses curve dramatically down to the smooth surface of the water. Their glittering lights reflect like a firework display on this sheltered lagoon. Dozens of triangular buildings float gently on the water, strung together by pedestrian walk-ways at first-floor level. All around us we see shopping centres, schools, churches and green parks. Sleek little water-buses dart about like dodgems at a fair.

The air is clean and fresh as we walk from the ferry to one of the fast elevators that will take us up to our new home—a seven-room flat built high into the inside of the outer concrete wall. But it is a flat with a difference—quite unlike any-

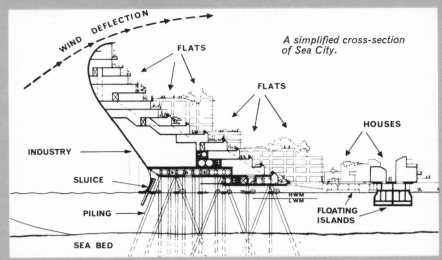

A simplified cross-section of Sea City.

Below: Sea City would even have its own football stadium (to background) and a Marine Zoo (floating, wedge-shaped buildings, to foreground).

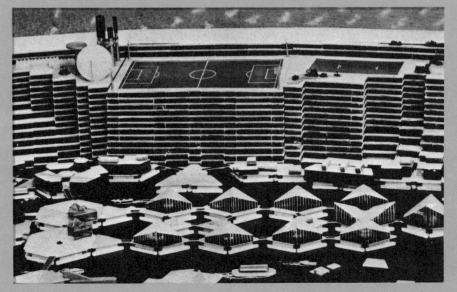

thing that we have seen on the mainland. One wall is built entirely of reinforced glass—giving us a fantastic view of the city. There is even a garden of our own in which to relax and sunbathe in complete privacy. Automation is complete; air-conditioning, central heating, TV in every room . . . There's even an automatic waste-removal system to save Mum the trouble of putting out a dustbin once a week. All she has to do is pop the rubbish down a chute in the kitchen and a conveyor-belt below takes it away silently.

It doesn't take us long to realize what a wonderful place Sea City is for young people. Take youth clubs. Instead of the dingy old hall we were used to on the mainland there are no less than eight spe-

cially designed youth centres, each one with full sport and entertainment facilities built in. There is a huge football stadium with covered-in seating for all spectators, built on top of the outer wall. (With a ground like this, Sea City United will be top of Division One in no time at all!) Then there are the water-sporting facilities. Fabulous! A huge boating-lake covers part of the inner lagoon, and there are special mooring points under the houses for our yachts and motor-boats.

On top of all this there are many public gardens, two theatres, a cinema, six churches and no less than fourteen restaurants. (There are also twenty-seven schools, but you don't want to know about those!) The biggest attraction of all is the Marine Zoo, an extraordinary place built half under the water, where we can watch strange creatures of the sea living in their natural conditions.

Sea City is a wonderful place for Mum and Dad, too. Gleaming shopping arcades span the south side of the city, all under cover so that Mum doesn't get wet when she's staggering home with the week's provisions on a rainy day. There's plenty of work close at hand for Dad. In the city itself are fish-farming plants, sand and ballast centres (these valuable building materials are dredged up from the ocean bed below), freshwater production plants and Marine Study Laboratories. If none of these suit him, Great Yarmouth—with its growing industry—is only a few minutes away by hoverferry.

Above: *The transportation area (foreground) would link Sea City with the mainland.*

Left: *Artist's impression of an inside view of Sea City, with islands and terraces.*

Life on Sea City sounds great, all right—but what about the howling gales and crashing waves that have made many a North Sea traveller never want to leave dry land again? Won't these things make life in Sea City impossible after all?

The answer is that they won't—for the architects who designed the city have learnt a lesson from the builders of medieval towns. Just as Sea City will be threatened from the outside by wind and waves, so towns in the Middle Ages were threatened by attacking armies. These armies were kept at bay by two lines of defence. The main one was a strong wall, twelve-foot thick and with firm foundations. In the same way, Sea City protects itself with that massive structure of reinforced concrete, specially curved to deflect the wind above it.

But the wall-builders of ancient times knew that one line of defence was not enough. However strong it was, attack after attack with a battering ram would eventually knock it down. So they devised a very clever way of limiting the force with which the attackers could strike their wall. They called it a *moat*.

In just the same way, the planners of Sea City knew that their wall of concrete would soon be brought down if the great waves were not checked before they crashed up against it. So they built a 20th-century version of the medieval moat.

All around the city, except for a gap to let ships through (just like a drawbridge), stretches a line of sausage-shaped canisters. These are positioned at some distance from the wall, and being part-filled with fresh water float low in the sea. They are enough to break the back of the giant waves coming crashing in, reducing them to harmless ripples by the time they reach the wall.

Oh, yes! Sea City *is* a possibility all right. It *could* be started tomorrow if the money were readily available.

Perhaps, during your lifetime, you will have the choice to live on the land—or to live on the sea. If you like fishing, sailing or swimming, then one day you might find yourself standing on the Great Yarmouth hoverferry terminal with a one-way ticket to Sea City!

Right: *The islands inside the lagoon would comprise of six triangles, each 120 feet long, with flood tanks to keep the sections level according to the building load carried.*

Below: *A cross-section of Sea City's wall, revealing the power complex.*

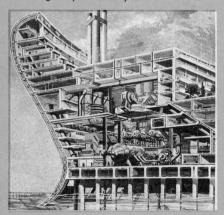

PLANET OF REJECTS

STAR TREK

THE STARSHIP 'ENTERPRISE' CONTINUED ITS EXPLORATION THROUGH THE UNCHARTED DEEP SPACE OF ASTRAL SECTOR IV. IT WAS THE VOICE OF COMMUNICATIONS OFFICER LIEUTENANT UHURA THAT BROKE THE CALM SILENCE OF THE COMMAND CENTRE...

CAPTAIN KIRK, SIR! ALIEN SHIP, BEARING FOUR-FORTY, GREEN!

LET'S HAVE IT ON THE TELE-VIDEO, LIEUTENANT!

THERE'S A PLANET ON THE EDGE OF THE SECTOR. LOOKS LIKE THAT'S HER DESTINATION!

WHAT DO YOU MAKE OF IT, MR. SPOCK?

COURSE TRACKERS KEPT THE SHIP IN VIEW...

TYPE UNKNOWN. CROSSING OUR COURSE... IT'S STRANGE THAT SHE'S IGNORING US...

BUT SHE'S GOING STRAIGHT INTO THE ATMOSPHERE – SPEED UNCHECKED!

IT HAPPENED SUDDENLY – INEVITABLY. THE SHIP HIT THE FRICTION DENSITY OF THE UPPER LAYERS...

NO, SULU – NO PISTOL TACTICS YET. LET'S FIND OUT WHO THEY ARE...

THE AUTOMATIC TRANSLATOR/COMMUNICATOR SOLVED THE LANGUAGE PROBLEM...

WE MEAN YOU NO HARM. WE'RE ON A PEACEFUL MISSION FROM THE PLANET EARTH!

THEN IT IS WELL YOU LANDED HERE. I AM KANDOK, CAPTAIN OF A SHIP FROM THAX THAT CRASHED HERE SIX MONTHS AGO. THIS IS MY CREW...

WITHOUT RADIO, WITH LITTLE FOOD, WE WERE PREPARED TO DIE HERE, STRANDED!

THEN YOUR WORRIES ARE OVER, FRIEND. WE'LL TAKE YOU BACK TO YOUR PLANET!

ABOARD 'ENTERPRISE' SPECIAL QUARTERS WERE MADE READY FOR THE ALIENS...

HOPE YOU'LL BE COMFORTABLE, KANDOK. CAN YOU GIVE ME A COURSE FOR THAX?

CERTAINLY. WE WILL GO TO YOUR COMMAND CENTRE?

AND SO...

THE CALCULATIONS ARE QUITE SIMPLE...

PERHAPS YOU'D LIKE ME TO CONTACT THAX AND GIVE THEM THE GOOD NEWS OF YOUR RESCUE?

IT WAS THEN THAT KANDOK MOVED – TOO SWIFTLY FOR KIRK TO STOP HIM...

THERE WILL BE **NO** COMMUNICATIONS, CAPTAIN!

WHAT THE HECK...?

SWIFTLY, KIRK AND THE OTHERS WERE DISARMED...

WE WERE NOT CRASH VICTIMS. WE WERE **EXILED** TO THAT PLANET FROM THAX. CONDEMNED TO PERISH AS REBELS AGAINST OUR GOVERNMENT!

KIRK FELT A HAND SEIZE HIS ARM FROM BEHIND, AND HIS FOOT WHIPLASHED BACKWARDS...

SPOCK! GET KANDOK!

AAAGH!

IN ONE INSTANT, BOTH KIRK AND SPOCK LEARNED THAT THE ALIENS POSSESSED FEARFUL STRENGTH...

UUGGH!

YOU FOOLS! DO YOU THINK YOU CAN DEFY THE MIGHT OF KANDOK?

GUHH!

THE AGONY OF THE BLOW SEEPED SLOWLY FROM KIRK'S BODY...

NOW, CAPTAIN, YOU WILL OBEY ME IMPLICITLY. THE GIRL IS MY HOSTAGE. ONE FALSE MOVE OF ANY KIND AND SHE DIES!

HELPLESS, KIRK COULD DO NOTHING BUT HAND OVER CONTROL AND FORBID THE CREW TO ATTEMPT RETALIATION...

LOCK THOSE TWO UP! THEY'RE DANGEROUS— THE GIRL STAYS IN HERE WITH US!

SIMPLE IN THEORY, IT WAS EVEN SIMPLER IN PRACTICE...

TWO GAS GRENADES WILL BE ENOUGH. LET'S GET THESE MASKS ON AND DROP THEM IN!

HAND 'EM UP. THEY SHOULD TAKE FIVE SECONDS!

PINS PULLED, THE CHEMICAL 'EGGS' ROLLED ON THEIR WAY...

NOW!

BUT AS THE DOOR CRASHED OPEN...

MY STARS! IT HASN'T AFFECTED THEM! THEY'RE IMMUNE!

THE MOMENT OF FROZEN SURPRISE ON BOTH SIDES LASTED ONLY A SPLIT SECOND...

CUT THEM DOWN!

ONE OF KANDOK'S MEN LEAPT FORWARD, BUT...

DIE, INTERFERING FOOL!

NOT YET, FRIEND!

Y'IEEEE!

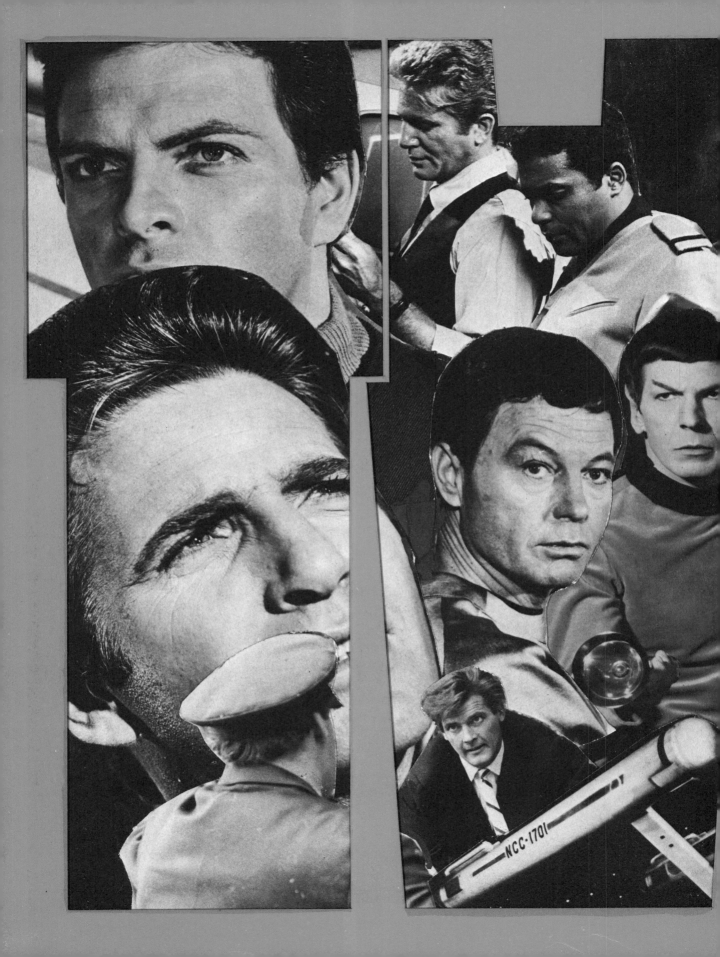